Overcoming the Lie of "Race"

A Personal, Philosophical, and Political Perspective

ALSO BY JOHN L. HODGE

BOOKS

Dialogues on God: Three Views (2012)

How We Are Our Enemy—And How to Stop: Our Unfinished Task of Fulfilling the Values of Democracy (2011)

Cultural Bases of Racism and Group Oppression: An Examination of Traditional "Western" Concepts, Values and Institutional Structures Which Support Racism, Sexism and Elitism (co-author) (1975)

BOOK CHAPTERS:

"Equality: Beyond Dualism and Oppression," Chapter 6 of *Anatomy of Racism* (1990)

"Democracy and Free Speech: A Normative Theory of Society and Government," Chapter 5 of *The First Amendment Reconsidered* (1982)

JOURNAL ARTICLE:

"Deadlocked-Jury Mistrials, Lesser Included Offenses, and Double Jeopardy: A Proposal to Strengthen the Manifest Necessity Requirement," *Criminal Justice Journal* (Vol. 9, No. 1) (1986)

FOR DETAILS, GO TO HTTP://JOHN L. HODGE.COM

Overcoming the Lie
of "Race"

A PERSONAL, PHILOSOPHICAL, AND POLITICAL PERSPECTIVE

John L. Hodge
J.D., Ph.D.

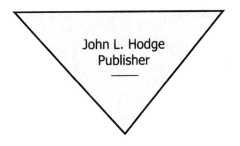

John L. Hodge
Publisher

Published in the U.S.A,
by
John L. Hodge, Publisher
Jamaica Plain, Massachusetts
U.S.A.
JLHPublisher@gmail.com

Cover design by John L. Hodge.

Your comments are appreciated. Use the email address above.
Order books from local or online retailers.

For more information,
go to the website at
http://johnlhodge.com

ISBN: 978-0-9831790-5-4

Print on demand services provided by Lightning Source, Inc.

Printed copies available through
local and online bookstores.
Check for ebook availability.

CONTENTS

PREFACE

What if you had just learned that something you fully believed, something quite important that had shaped your life, was false?

Had you been deceived? How would you have lived differently had you known? What would you do now?

And how would you handle this revelation if everyone else you knew was certain that what you realized was false was true? Why would they believe you if you told them what you know now? Wouldn't they dismiss you as someone not to be believed, as someone who was perhaps a nut?

I learned as a child—from my own observations because no one told me directly—that what most people believed about "race" was false. I was what was called then a "Negro," something that was supposed to determine how I lived and what I could do. It seemed that everyone believed that being a "Negro" was an unchangeable biological trait that necessarily would determine my future.

Yet, even though this was consciously believed, and no one said anything directly to question it, no one in my extended family acted as though being "Negro" meant any kind of inferiority. I absorbed what they thought without a word of explanation.

But in addition, I knew something else—which perhaps they knew too but did not express—that any line drawn that separated "whites" from "Negroes" was false.

Many will think that calling the idea of "race" a "lie" is too strong. Isn't it just a myth? A reasonable error? Lies require liars.

I think the facts that I present in this book point to the need for the stronger term. Perpetuating the idea of "race" when it was known to be false has required intentional deception. I have concluded, based on the historical facts, that the appropriate term is "lie." I will not lie to you about it and gloss over what appears to me to be the stark truth.

Historian Jacqueline Jones calls the myth of "race" "a dreadful deceit." She says that the idea of "race" is a fiction "contrived for specific political purposes."[1] In other words, a lie.

I was fortunate in that I could deal with this from an early age. It was not some discovery late in life that might have shocked me into the despair of believing that my past life had been misguided or wasted, or some crazy idea that must be false because everyone knew that it could not be true, or an idea so shocking that I would have to deny it to maintain the legitimacy of how I had lived.

In short, I knew from a young age that the idea that a biological line could be drawn between "white" and "Negro" was a lie. How did I live among others who either believed the lie to be true, or if they knew it was a lie, chose not to let on that they knew? But pretending not to know is also a lie.

This book is about how I handled this lie. But that still does not explain why I chose to write this book.

I think that is explained by the values I grew up with, but I cannot be sure. These are values I absorbed without a word being spoken.

My family valued honesty and scientific validity. My father was a scientist. My mother was educated to be a scientist. My paternal grandfather was a science teacher. The importance of this orientation towards science is that ideas and beliefs had to be connected to facts. (I discuss this further in Chapter 8.) Anything could be subject to question. The result was an environment of healthy skepticism.

In addition, many in my extended family, including the scientists, were people who sought to improve the lives of others. They were teachers, social workers, journalists and activists. From them I learned the importance of a broader social and political perspective.

There was also a third element that I only recently recognized. In my family, anger was rarely expressed. That did not prevent me as a child from having occasional tantrums, but I was always gently guided towards the family norm of suppressed expression of anger. The norm was to treat any problem giving rise to negative emotions as something to fix. In short, "If it makes you angry, do not express anger; instead, fix it."

This, of course, was never directly expressed, but it is the way my family behaved.

In their various occupations, they were in positions to fix things. My father was a food chemist working to fix the spoiling of foods; his sister was a social worker working to fix, among other things, the care of unmarried mothers and their children, and later, the health care of an urban county; her first husband died of a heart attack trying to fix the policing of a major city; her second husband became a state legislator to fix state-wide problems; as a high school principal, my grandfather worked to fix the level of education in his community. My grandmother was constantly at the sewing machine mending and making this and that. When my grandfather came home, he fixed other people's radios, the main means of connecting to the world in those days. Most people just got angry at them when they broke. I was told that his father, my grandfather's father, was a freelance mechanic who fixed broken machinery. I am sure my mother would have fixed things too had she not succumbed too young to illness. When my father retired, he worked to fix golf clubs so they would perform better. As a chemist, he even sought to fix a medical problem that prevented medication from entering his liver to suppress the cancer growing there. Everyone around me was trying to fix something, day and night.

Thus, I am writing this book as part of my family tradition: Question beliefs with facts; work to benefit others; and if something makes me angry, fix it.

Racism is wrong. It is a societal sickness. It is contradicted by facts. It makes me angry. I want to fix it, but I cannot fix it by myself. I write in the hope that I can rally your support to fix it.

In this book I will often describe my own experiences. I do not assume, and the reader should not assume, that my experiences in any way invalidate the experiences of anyone else. My experiences occurred in particular places at particular times. They probably would have been different in other places or at other times. But this does not diminish the validity of what I experienced.

"The legacy of the past racism directed at blacks in the United States is more like a bacillus that we have failed to destroy, a live germ that not only continues to make some of us ill but retains the capacity to generate new strains of a disease for which we have no certain cure."
—George M. Fredrickson, *Racism: A Short History* (2002), p. 143.

"Racism is, and always has been, the way America has sorted and ranked its people in a bitterly divisive, humanity-robbing system."
—Debby Irving, *Waking Up White* (2014), p. 31.

"'Race' itself is a fiction, one that has no basis in biology or any long-standing, consistent usage in human culture."
Jacqueline Jones, *A Dreadful Deceit* (2013), p. x

INTRODUCTION

All you require to expose a lie is to observe without bias, to see without the intrusion of interpretation.

Sometimes, when I concentrate or am unusually relaxed, my eyes see what they see free of preconceptions and societal influences. This does not always happen.

When it happens, and I just look at someone from a distance, the first thing I usually notice is the person's bodily profile, including height and body shape. I notice whether the person is tall or short, skinny or fat, and the sizes in between. Then, almost immediately, a conceptualization intrudes that classifies the person as male or female. But my eyes do not see male or female. Male or female is a classification that comes from my mind. That it comes from my mind is clear when occasionally I see someone who is not easily classified. When that happens, my mind gets befuddled, but my eyes continue to see what they see without regard to classifying gender; the mental classification gets put on hold.

Just as quickly another conceptualization intrudes and the idea of "race" imposes itself. That idea leads us to put people into "racial" categories. The details of the person in a "racial" category then get replaced by conceptual generalizations of that person's "race," particularly if that person is categorized as of another "race." The idea of "race" is so powerful that it interferes with further perception, replacing perception with conceptualization. "Race can reduce the accuracy of eyewitness identifications; a witness is statistically less likely to identify correctly a suspect of another race."[2] Once identified as an "other," the other's details no longer matter. Thus, to see the details accurately, we have to see without the intrusion of "racial" categories.

When I occasionally see without "racial" categorization, I often wonder why the "races" of humankind were not divided up differently. Tall people and short people are clearly different types, as are those with wide frames and those with slim frames. Considering these features that I often notice first, a tall, slim "white" person and a tall, slim "black" person would be the same "race."

It's fun to rearrange things mentally. When I compare professional American football players with basketball players, I see two different "races." The bodily profiles of typical "white" football players look much more like typical "black" football players than they look like typical "white" basketball players who look more like typical "black" basketball players. So there should be a football "race" and a basketball "race." This seems as sensible to me as basing "race" on skin color.

Of course, I notice skin color, though I often wonder if I have been culturally conditioned to pay special attention to it. But I also notice facial shapes, how some people regardless of "race" have round faces and some narrow faces; some have shallow rounded chins, and others have long pointed chins. Black hair and blond hair are quite noticeably different. Some have straight hair that could be of any color, and some have curly hair that could be of any color.

A person with curly black hair, a rounded face and receding chin, and a short, slim body might be "white" or "black" depending solely on a relatively slight difference in skin color. Two such people of the same age and weight would look more alike than different. They would look more alike than if their skin color would classify them both as "white" but one was a blond and the other a brunette. That the accepted "racial" differences seem to matter more than other differences strikes me as odd. Why are these "racial" differences so important as to dominate how we see people?

This is not just theoretical. Recently I walked in my Boston neighborhood of Jamaica Plain past a tall, slim woman talking to a tall, slim man only slightly taller than the woman. Their attractive, athletic bodies were remarkably similar, and that was what I noticed first. As I passed by I saw that their pleasant, smiling faces had similar oval shapes. The man had medium brown skin and thus was "black." The woman had light skin and fairly straight hair and thus was "white." To me, they looked very much alike.

Even more recently I was sitting in a restaurant with my wife. My seat faced the window looking out onto the street near the center of a town northwest of Boston within the Greater Boston metropolitan area. It was a lovely but slightly chilly spring day following a horribly brutal winter. I saw two pre-teenage girls half walking and half skipping toward us, both the same height and with nearly identical slim bodies. As they approached, they seemed very much alike. Their interaction suggested joy and friendship. As they got closer, I noticed that one of the girls had very dark skin and hair tied in a bun on top of her head. Then I noticed that the other girl had very light skin, and as she passed, I saw her long blond hair dropping below her shoulders. As they walked-skipped away, I still thought they looked much more alike than different.

My advancing age has not diminished my regarding some women as physically attractive and some as less so. I am quite aware that far more important than outward appearance is a person's character, personality and values, but these important things are not what first gets my attention. I have noticed that my response to physical attractiveness has nothing to do with "race." So why are "racial" differences relevant at all?

When I stood inside the restaurant where I saw the two girls passing by, waiting for my wife to come from the bathroom before we left, I saw the young woman sitting at the table that had been next to us and was struck by the breath-taking symmetrical beauty of her face. Previously I had only glanced sideways at her while she and her male friend spoke a language I did not understand. I did not want to intrude by staring or taking her picture, but I wished I could have had a longer look. Her rounded face and slanted eyes revealed Asian ancestry. We were in a Korean restaurant. It was just another example of how beauty and what we think of as "race" are unrelated.

That "race" is irrelevant to physical attraction seems to be quite widespread. When the English and Africans encountered each other in the New World four centuries ago, there was plenty of sex between them. In the decades that followed those early encounters, there was enough sex between them that laws were passed to prevent it, unsuccessfully. There would have been no need for such laws if there were not mutual attractions. This cross-group sex was not all due to physical coercion, as is widely believed. Physically coercive sex certainly happened, but there were also marriages and many other cooperative relationships. The first laws in early colonial America that futilely attempted to ban these relationships punished only the English women who voluntarily engaged in them.

The results of these many relationships were many children. What "race" were they? Similar sexual relationships occurred between Europeans and indigenous Americans ("Indians" or "Native Americans") and between indigenous Americans and Africans and mixed African-Europeans. These relationships too produced many children. What "race" were they? Today we talk about "interracial" marriages and "mixed-race" children as though this is something different from the norm, but these American mixtures have been occurring for four centuries. (More details follow in Chapter 4.)

My observations about "race" began when I was a child, for reasons that will become evident in Chapter 1. These observations led me to the conclusion that there is no biological, scientific or sensible basis for the idea of "race." Many already know this, but nonetheless they still talk about "race" as though it is biologically real. They still see "races" when they see people, even if they'll say that they do not believe "races" really exist.

It is necessary to talk about the prevalent false beliefs about "race." To do this without reaffirming the false beliefs, I put "racial" terms in quotation marks to indicate that we are talking about what people falsely believe. The quotation marks mean "so-called": called so falsely. The quotation marks punctuate what we write. But they should also punctuate how we think. When we think about "race," we should think in quotation marks. This book will explain why.

Exposing the lie of "race" is not to say that we do not observe physical differences correlated with culture and geographic origins. Such differences are obvious, but "racial" terms are both too broad and too narrow to capture these correlations.

For example, I have noticed that "white" people in different cities in the United States differ significantly from one another. The "white" people of Boston (where I have lived for the latter half of my life), on the whole, do not look or behave quite the same as "white" people in, say, Seattle. There is overlap, but there are also observable differences in the distributions of traits for things like hair curliness and facial shapes. The cultures of these two liberal northern U.S. cities, both approximately the same size, are also different, overlapping but with different ambiances. Thus, to simply say all these people are "white" is to ignore differences and treat them as alike. Furthermore, "white" people in some communities in the Boston area even look different from "white" people in other communities in and around Boston. Again, the distributions of observable traits are different. Even the style of lawns and gardens differ from one predominantly "white" community to another, reflecting cultural and sometimes religious differences. Why are these different cultural communities not different "races"? Why are these cultural differences any different from the cultural differences we think exists between different recognized "races"?

The cultural differences between, say, Boston and Seattle, while quite observable, are nonetheless tiny compared to the differences between Boston and any politically conservative city. So a strong case could be made that the people of Boston of all colors are a different culture from the people of, say, Phoenix or Oklahoma City. If significant cultural differences imply "racial" differences, then the "white" people of these different places are different "races."

One could also make the case, based on very prominent cultural and political differences that are often reflected in observable demeanor and facial expressions, that Republicans and Democrats are two different "races." They tend to work in different places and live in different cities.[3] Even their shopping and eating habits are different.[4] When surveyed about their views of "racial" justice, "white"

Republicans and "white" Democrats were far apart while "white" Democrats and "blacks" had more overlap than differences.[5] Culturally, if comparing people who have similar education, economic status, and locality, Republicans differ from Democrats quite significantly while "white" Democrats differ from "black" Democrats relatively little.

The distinctions that we do make based on "race" are the product of history, culture, and lies. These distinctions are based on a concept of "race" that consists of the "assigning of fixed or permanent differences among human descent groups."[6] This idea of unchangeable differences resulted in "the modern concept of races as basic human types classified by physical differences (primarily skin color)."[7] Such fixed or permanent differences of human groups do not exist. To say that they do exist in spite of known evidence showing this to be false is the lie I speak of.

"Racial" distinctions have political origins. As we know, politics and truth do not always intersect. "Racial" distinctions were (i) imposed by those in power, (ii) placed into laws enforced by the power of state and local governments, (iii) initially incorporated implicitly into the U.S. Constitution, and (iv) upheld by national legislation and the U.S. Supreme Court until the middle of the twentieth century. These distinctions gave some people lower social status than others, distinctions that for over two centuries in America often made the difference between a master and a slave. Even after slavery ended, these distinctions usually determined where one could live, what jobs were available, and whom one could legally marry.

"Racial" distinctions are important in societies that retain and seek to preserve hierarchical orderings based on status and class—societies that, because of this and other factors, have not become complete democracies. We live in an incomplete democracy, a place where people are not equal. We live in a society that is still far from fulfilling the ideals upon which it is based. One major impediment to fulfilling these ideals is the lie of "race." "Racial" classifications create artificial dividing lines that separate us into different categories. The effect of these classifications is to place impediments in the road to each individual's full use of his or her abilities to attain individually determined goals and aspirations. The society as a whole suffers as a consequence.

The lie of "race," due to its long history, affects the present. The lie has shaped history—though, unfortunately, it is not the only lie to have done so. We cannot just close our eyes to it. To pretend that history has not been so shaped is to pretend that that the lie never happened. The lie cannot be simply ignored without passively allowing its harmful historical effects to continue. To be fair to people disadvantaged and advantaged by this historical lie, we have to continue our awareness of the "racial" distinctions that have been made. This is necessary to repair the persistent damage that the lie has caused.

But in recognizing these "racial" distinctions as lies, we also rise to a higher level of consciousness. With this higher level of consciousness, we value others and personally relate to others without regard to "race" while recognizing that we have all been adversely affected by the lie of "race." In this sense we become post-racial but not post-"racial." We become post-racial by recognizing that "race" is a lie and by relating to others without being confined by it. But we do not become post-"racial" in that we recognize the harm the lie has caused and continues to cause. In other words, the idea of *race* is false, but "race"—what people falsely believe—is real.

Although I focus here primarily on the United States, racism and correlates of racism—especially religious ones—exist all over the world. Beliefs in the "racial" superiority of one's own group or nationality are significant factors among the causes of war.[8] I focus on the United States, because I have lived here all of my life. I also focus more on the distinction between "black" and "white," because that is the distinction that I am most familiar with and that has had the most impact on my life.

This focus is not intended to ignore or belittle racism against other non-"whites," including the people we call "Latinos," "Native Americans," and "Asians." That racism has also been brutal and murderous.[9]

I also focus on the United States, because it has been one of the most racist parts of the world since the seventeenth century. Unlike much of the world that is nonetheless full of prejudice and hatred for the "other," racism in the United States until the middle of the twentieth century was enforced by the laws and power of governments, particularly—but not only—in the former slave states of the American South. Due to this combination of state-enforced and publicly supported racism, historian George M. Fredrickson placed the southern United States during the long "Jim Crow" era that emerged after the Civil War in the same category as South Africa under apartheid and Nazi Germany. He groups these three together, because "nowhere else were the political and legal potentialities of racism so fully realized."[10] (Anyone who thinks this is an exaggeration should read the succinct overview of Jim Crow in the 1900s in Chapter 1 of *The Pursuit of Fairness: A History of Affirmative Action*, by Terry H. Anderson.)[11] The widespread practice of segregation outside of the South along with the tacit and often explicit acceptance of the South's apartheid laws incriminated the northern United States as well. As a noted journalist stated in 1964, "The history of the Negro in the North is stained with prejudice."[12]

Although legally supported overt racism in the United States has ended, the legacy of this racism is still evident throughout the country, even more so in the southern states where the legacy of slavery is the strongest, where the Confederacy and its history of slavery, segregation and racism are still honored.[13] Racism will remain evident until we make appropriate repairs and also rid ourselves of the lie of "race."

What has been too little recognized is that this racist heritage oppressed many "whites" as well as "blacks" and other non-"whites." "Whites" who did not agree with legalized segregation were nonetheless forced by law to comply. Nothing separated "blacks" from "whites" more completely than the laws against "interracial" marriages.[14] These laws, upheld by the nation's highest court, were blatant intrusions by government into the intimate personal lives and liberty of both "whites" and their non-"white" partners.[15] Both partners suffered the same prohibitions and the same penalties.[16] "Whites" were also oppressed by other "whites" when, in the early nineteenth century before the Civil War, many southern states instituted laws that prevented "whites" from freeing their slaves as many had previously done.[17] These laws took away the liberty of "whites" to repudiate slavery as well as the potential liberty of slaves. Many "whites" who joined the 1960s civil rights movement in the South were brutalized, and some were killed—by other "whites."

Thus, legalized racism was a not only a means of oppressing "blacks" and other non-"whites" but was also an exercise of political power that oppressed "whites" who did not agree with racist practices. "White" ministers who willingly performed cross-"race" marriages were also oppressed by the laws that later made their involvement a crime. Legalized racism was not simply a conflict of "white" against "black" and other non-"whites," it was also a conflict of some "whites" with economic and political power (often a minority) and their allies against other dissenting "whites" who had less power.

We need to think differently about our similarities and differences. A political difference exists between—for lack of better terminology— conservatives whose policies are indifferent to or increase inequality, and liberals who favor equality. This is a difference between those who seek treatment of others as equals and those who favor hierarchical arrangements that benefit some at the expense of others. This difference is worldwide and seems to exist within every country and within every ethnic group.

This difference is one of values. Similarity of values can cross over all other distinctions. It is a more important similarity than that of "race," ethnicity, nationality or religion. These cross-group similarities connect people who may be oppressed minorities in their own societies with others who may be a part of a world-wide emergence of more democratic and peaceful ways of thinking. For this connection to actually happen, we will need to recognize and reach out to others with similar values without regard to other distinctions.

Overcoming racism and recognizing the lie of "race" are important ingredients in the worldwide struggle for equality, though this is only part of the struggle. The future holds the promise of greater equality for all, but the hierarchical past holds us back. Racism and the very idea of "race" are parts of this past holding us back.

PART I

PERSONAL ENCOUNTERS WITH A SOCIAL LIE

Chapter 1

Through the Eyes of a Child

Although I did not see my birth certificate until I was fully grown, what it says is a good introduction to my childhood. It indicates that I was born in 1939 in Lawrence, Kansas. On the certificate is a place for designating the "race or color" of my parents. In the space for my father, there is a "C." The same "C" appears in the space for my mother. "C" stood for "colored."

"Colored" then meant what was also called "Negro," and "Negro" was later replaced by "black" and then "African American." To be "colored" then meant the same thing as being "black" or "African American" today, namely, "not white." It did not matter that "white" is also a color, that people called "white" range from pink to tan, and that only dead people could actually come close to being white.

So what colors counted as being "colored"? And what was I? Although my birth certificate is silent about my "race or color," it would be presumed that if my mother and father were "colored," then I must be "colored."

So what "color" were they? By father was light to medium brown, depending on how much golf he played. My mother was medium brown but darker than my father. My mother died from illness when I was quite young, so I only know what she looked like from photographs. The antibiotics that would have cured her had not yet become available to the public.

So what "color" was I? I was a tannish light brown, marginally lighter than my father. That meant that I was lighter, just barely, than my parents. That seemed to be of no significance to anyone, since most around me had seen this kind of thing before, especially since there were others in my family who were much lighter than I was.

I remember one day when several family members and friends had an animated discussion about my eye color. I wondered, why did it matter? What was all the excitement about? I do not remember my exact age when this happened, but I was probably around five or six. Some thought my eyes were blue, others thought they were gray. The consensus seemed to be that they were gray. I looked in the mirror and they seemed gray to me, with a bluish tinge. I had no idea then why there seemed to be any emotion attached to this merely factual observation. My grandfather had grayish-light-brownish eyes, as I recall. My father's eyes were brown. Apparently my eyes were a little different from everyone else's. In nearly every other respect, I looked like a perfect blend of my father and my mother.

No one said much about my hair, which fit in well with other family members. It was curly, but a little less curly than my father's. Since my grandfather had straight hair, having hair that was less curly than my parents was not remarkable.

When I speak of my grandparents, I refer only to my paternal grandparents. I do not remember having any contact with my mother's parents. After my mother died, I lived with my grandparents. I considered them to be my mother and father, plus I also had a father who lived elsewhere but visited frequently. So in practice I had two fathers. Fortunately they got along. Conflict within the family was rare. If it occurred, they kept me protected from it.

It was growing up with my grandparents, particularly my grandfather, where my thoughts about "race" were provoked.

At this point I need to clarify my terminology, since the terms "Negro" and "colored" used then are no longer considered acceptable. In my view, it does not matter which of the current terms I use: "black" or "African American." They are equally false identifiers, which is why I put these terms in quotation marks. I do not think one term is better than the other. However, "black" has the virtue of being short, crisp, and easier to write.

My grandmother was clearly not "white." Her skin was somewhere between medium and light brown. Had she been as light-skinned as two of her five sisters, she could have been mistaken for "white." Her hair, a blend of wavy and frizzy but not intensely curly, would not have prevented the mistake—a "mistake," that is, from the perspective of social norms. Her facial shape could have been found anywhere in the world—Europe, Asia, Africa—though I did not see that until later, as I knew nothing of the world as a child. As an adult, I once saw an elderly Asian woman whose face reminded me of my grandmother.

It was my grandfather who could raise eyebrows and might make "whites" wonder why he was with this "black" woman. "Blacks" would assume he was "black" because of his wife, for they were usually familiar with "white"-looking "blacks." But they would not make that assumption if he was alone outside of the segregated "black" community of Kansas City, Kansas.

He had light off-white skin similar to that of people called "white," straight hair, thin lips, and a long-chinned face that was within the range of "whites." As a child, I sometimes wondered if he was "white." But at some point I was shown a picture of his father, and he was clearly "black" with medium-brown skin. My grandfather considered himself "black" (i.e., "colored," "Negro") and lived as a "black" man, with an exception that I explain below.

His mother looked quite "white." She appeared in a photograph that hung on a living room wall. I did not ask whether she was "white," but assumed that she was probably as "black" as my grandfather. My aunt, however, told me several years ago that she had asked her father, "Was she white?" My grandfather's response was a somewhat ambiguous denial that she could be anything but "black." Normally he spoke carefully and precisely. My aunt remembered the ambiguity and continued to wonder if my great-grandmother was "white."

We may never know, especially since laws about who was "white" and who was "black" changed over time and differed from one state to another. Of course, the question is about what people thought, not about any biological reality. As told in the 1927 musical *Show Boat,*[18] that exposed some of the absurdity of "racial" prejudice; in many states you were "colored" if you had a drop of "colored blood." (I saw this musical at the Starlight Theater in Kansas City, Missouri when I was a teenager.) A drop would not necessarily change anyone's appearance.

To be in a family where my biological relations ranged from "white"-looking to medium-brown was not strange to me. The darkest skins in my extended family as well as some of the lightest skins were distributed among my grandmother's eleven brothers and sisters. In my "black" community, other "blacks" had similar ranges of coloring, even within the same family.

I knew one such family well. For a few years my closest friend, who I will call "Tom," was slightly lighter than me, like his mother. His maternal grandfather's skin was the color of milk chocolate, darker than anyone in my family. Tom's sister's skin color was the same as her grandfather's. Tom's grandmother looked "white."

There were also families whose members were all very light-skinned. At school, there was a full range of skin colors among students and teachers, from dark chocolate to looking "white." We were all "black." What this range of coloring meant became clear to me in my tenth grade biology class, which I will get to soon.

A few years before that class something happened that made me think about "race."

One day my grandfather left on a Saturday afternoon. Where was he going? My grandmother said he was going to the movies. I asked what was playing at the Princess Theater, the only movie theater in Kansas City, Kansas that admitted "blacks." She said that he was not going there but to another theater that happened to be in the "white" part of town. I asked how he could go there, and my grandmother said that since he looked "white" he could go there and that he needed to get away to relax. After that, I did not ask where he went to the movies, which he did occasionally, since I knew he was not going to the Princess. Somehow I also understood why he could not get away to relax by staying within our community, because he had been the high school principal for so long that nearly everyone in our community recognized him. I understood the need to be alone, unrecognized. I was an only child, and being alone, often in my own room, was the unquestioned norm for me.

Ever since that happened, I began to wonder: How many "whites" were like my grandfather?

Since being "white" was a choice my grandfather occasionally made so he could go to "white" movie theaters, surely some like him made the choice to be "white" for all purposes. Not everyone, faced with the choice of being "white" or "black," would choose to be "black." I do not know why my grandfather made the choice that he did. I do know that he did not like deception, and to be "white" when his father and perhaps his mother were "black" would have required, given the times, a deception that he would reject. But I knew that not everyone was like that.

After that, whenever I saw a "white" person, I wondered if that person was "black" like my grandfather.

My grandfather was not the only one in my family or in my community who could be mistaken for "white." My aunt was light enough that she was sometimes thought to be "white." She and her second husband once told a story of arriving in a major city (Chicago, as I recall) and getting a taxi from the airport to their hotel. There were then two hotels in the city with the same name, one in the "black" part of town and one in the "white" part of town. The taxi driver first headed for the "black" one, then turned towards the "white" one. Upon reflection later, I thought that he must have been wondering, "Is this a white woman with a black lover ('white' hotel), or is this a black man with a white lover ('black' hotel)"? When they realized his confusion, they directed him to the "black" one.

There were other stories too that I heard as a child and remembered. My aunt's first husband (who died of a heart attack at a relatively young age) had the features of a "white" man except for his medium brown skin. He had many stories to tell about his many travels, where sometimes others wondered what he was. Once he said he lied to avoid the consequences. His sister's skin color was the same as that of many "white" people, but she rarely traveled so had no stories to tell—at least, none that I heard.

These stories built a foundation in my brain for the conclusion that prejudice based on skin color was silly and wrong. People could not really tell where the dividing line was between "white" and "black."

For a while in high school I dated a girl whose mother was brown-skinned "black" and her father "white." They lived in the "black" neighborhood of Kansas City, Missouri. No one could tell from looking at her that she had any "black" ancestry. Her brother also looked "white."

I was surprised when my grandmother told me, when I was in my mid-teens, not to be prejudiced toward my aunt's new boyfriend (who became my aunt's second husband) due to his darkness, since, she said, he seemed like a very nice and intelligent person. It helped that he was a Cornell graduate. The thought had not registered with me until then that one might think differently about other "blacks" based on their skin color. This seemed as wrong as the distinction between "black" and "white."

Obviously it did not make a difference to my aunt. Her friends came in all shades.

When my grandmother cautioned me against color prejudice, I remembered when, several years before, a dark-skinned classmate remarked that he was glad I could be friends with him since I was much lighter than he was. He was part of the migration from the South. When he said that, I dismissed the idea as silly and didn't think about it again until I heard my grandmother's guidance. I had never noticed or heard about color prejudice within our community except against "whites." I was not aware of anyone in my family entertaining prejudices against other "blacks" based on skin color.

If they had such prejudices, and perhaps they did, at least they did not consider them of enough significance to be talked about. My grandmother's words of caution were the only words I remember about color prejudice spoken in my family. But by speaking against color prejudice, my grandmother showed awareness that it existed.

Later, as a young adult, I was shocked to learn how widespread color prejudice was in many "black" communities. That made it clear to me that "blacks" could be as stupid as "whites." So I was immune to ideas that emerged later that "blacks" gained some special virtue from being oppressed.

So by the time I entered high school, I was quite aware that something was quite wrong about the idea of "race." I was critical when a chapter on "race" appeared in my tenth grade biology book.

The biology book presented classical "race" thinking as though it had been scientifically established. It showed drawings of the heads of the typical "Caucasian" (aka "white") male, "Negroid" (aka "black") male, "Indian" (aka "red") male, and Asian male. Since I was familiar only with "whites" and "blacks," my attention focused on them. The "white" man's facial side view showed a vertical profile, thin lips, whitish skin and straight hair. The "black" man's side view showed a slanted profile, thick lips, chocolate skin and intensely curly hair.

I sat toward the back of the 100% "black" class of about 25 people and looked at everyone. Only a few had skins as dark as book's "Negroid" male. Those with the darkest skin had facial profiles ranging from vertical to slanted, but less slanted than the book's "Negroid." None of them had lips quite as thick as the book's. There was only one person whose facial profile, including thick lips, closely resembled the book's "Negroid," but his skin was very light, and he had reddish hair. There was only one conclusion to draw: we were all a mixture of "white" and "black." (I did not know then that many also probably had ancestry from America's indigenous peoples.)

Our teacher—who I realized later was one of the best teachers I ever had except for this one day—spent one full class period on this one chapter. He presented the chapter in a straightforward way, repeating its content. It was the only day that he would not take questions from the class. He himself had very light skin, not unlike that of many considered to be "white," and facial features that were quite distinctive. He spent the class period talking about "races" as described in the book when he could not be classified as belonging to any of them. He spoke to a class consisting of no one who clearly fit the "racial" classifications. I still wonder what he was really thinking. The falsity of the chapter was observable, right before his very eyes and in front of every mirror.

I sensed that he knew that something was wrong, but he would not admit it in front of the class. I wondered if he felt that he was required to follow the book.

As explained later (Chapter 6), it was known many years before my tenth grade class that genetic traits did not combine into "racial" clumps. I knew nothing about this as a child. What was known was not revealed. By failing to mention what was known and presenting instead what had been refuted, the biology book's chapter on "race" was a lie.

The observable mixtures of physical traits that occurred in my community and within families provided an education in genetics. Physical traits were observable in every possible combination. Black skin, thin lips. Dark skin, natural straight hair. Light skin, thick lips. Facial profiles along a continuum and not connected to any other features. From observation I would see that physical traits did not come in "racial" clumps. Thus, I could see, just by observing, the same thing that scientists had confirmed many years before, and that Charles Darwin, based on his observations from around the world, recorded in 1871.[19] What I saw was not distinct "races" but multiple continuums and mixtures of different physical traits.

Couldn't others see what I saw?

My observations of twins were particularly illuminating. Of the several sets of twins who were my classmates, only one set was identical. Two sets of twins paired brothers of totally different skin colors. In both cases, one brother was dark and other very light. When my father had children after he remarried, two were twins, one light skinned, one medium brown slightly darker than my father. Their mother could pass for "white" (but did not). What I could see was that the skin color of children did not have to be a blend of the parents' skin colors or even fall between those of the parents. The same was true of other physical traits.

The biology book's chapter on "race" fed my growing awareness that there was a considerable gap between what people believed and what was true. My eyes saw what they saw. No one and no book could convince me that what I saw was false.

This awareness had a great influence on the rest of my life.

Chapter 2

"Race," Class, Region and Religion

My family's lighter skin colors posed no barriers to our participation in our "black" community. Skin colors like ours were prevalent throughout the community, so we were not unusual.

But I was aware that our circle of acquaintances included only a small part of the community. What separated us from the rest was class, education, region and religion. Being of the same "race" could not overcome these divisions.

I became more fully aware of the class divisions when I explored our community on foot looking for customers to buy the weekly *The Kansas City Call*, the "black"-owned newspaper from Kansas City, Missouri. This is how I earned extra spending money to finance my model railroad. Usually I knocked on the doors of houses that were similar to ours, modest-sized houses in good condition with yards. Most of the houses in our sub-neighborhood were like this, but mixed in among them was housing for those less well off. Next door to my house was a rooming house containing people whom we thought we had nothing in common with. Across the street was an apartment building containing people living in poverty. I played with a boy who lived there, but I could tell that my grandparents preferred that I not go there. Another house up the street was run down with an unkept yard. Many of the poor lived alongside of the middle class. There was some but not a lot of interaction between them.

Some sub-neighborhoods were entirely poor. I walked past them on the way to school. Some of my friends at school lived in them, and I sometimes visited them. Poverty there and then did not breed violence. There was no visible violence, no need for my grandparents to worry about my safety. On Friday nights I often walked a mile through a poor area to go the movies, and I walked alone. Throughout my childhood I remember only two classmates who had died, one in a car accident and another from illness. No child or teenager in my community died or was injured by guns or knives. The father of a friend was killed during a robbery of the father's liquor store. That is the only death by violence that I remember.

There was one very poor sub-neighborhood that was out of the way. I had no occasion to walk or ride through it on the way to something else. I ventured into it on foot trying to sell the *Call.* No one would buy it, probably because they could not afford it. I had no fear for my safety, but I felt that I was in an alien land among people I did not know and had no desire to know. Yet, I felt empathy for their situation. They seemed like decent people who happened to be poor. But I was clearly an outsider and did not belong there.

I wondered but did not confirm whether the people in this neighborhood had come from the South. I knew generally that southern "blacks" were moving northward. Occasionally our classes would be interrupted by new additions in the middle of the school year. The new additions were different. Their language was different. With some exceptions, they were not well educated. They formed their own subculture. The exceptions merged seamlessly with the rest of us.

As I was walking to school one day, I saw that a new small convenience store had opened in an old rundown building. I was in the tenth grade, attending the high school where my grandfather had been the principal before he retired. I went in and found a snack to purchase.

As I was checking out, the "black" clerk—who was probably the storeowner—asked me what I wanted to be when I grew up. I told him that I wanted to be an engineer. (I am not sure that he understood that I was not talking about driving a train.)

He said no, you cannot be an engineer. "Blacks" (whatever term he used) are not allowed to do that. You should be a doctor.

I was too surprised to explain that my father was steadily employed as a chemist by the U.S. Department of Agriculture, and that if he could be a chemist, I could be an engineer. I concluded that the clerk must be from the South and not know any better.

My mind churned from this encounter. He was telling me to stay in my place, the place where "blacks" belonged. Instead of working against racism, he had not only accepted it, he also assumed that insurmountable "racial" barriers existed where they did not. By accepting the barriers that he thought existed, he was not only limiting himself by subordinating himself to "white" prejudice, he was telling others to do the same. He was a "black" man telling other "blacks" to submit. It was a shocking thought.

Thereafter I wondered to what extent this internalized racism was affecting all of us. The clerk might be only an extreme example of something more common. From then on I realized that there were two forms of racism: that imposed by "whites" on "blacks" and that imposed by "blacks" on themselves. (I explore this further in Chapter 7.)

This meant that I had to be observant and critical of my own surroundings. Were other things going on that reflected the attitudes of the clerk? What thoughts, ideas and habits reflected self-assurance and which ones reflected self-imposed limitations?

That I had to be critical of my own surroundings was not something new, but the encounter with the clerk enhanced and expanded a critical attitude had been with me for a long time. I think I became critical long before the tenth grade.

I remember how critical I was of church. My grandparents belonged and attended services every Sunday morning. I had to come too. Its members were mixed middle-class and poor. Many were elderly. The church services always reached a high point when the minister gradually built up to a rhythmical poetic climax. That part I liked. What I did not like was the few who would loudly wail and moan. Although the singing was often beautiful, it was usually about suffering and pain. As a child, this was of no interest to me. I wanted to say something like, "Get over it and move on." But the complainers were probably too old to move on. I hoped that I would never get like that.

My grandparents sat stoically through these proceedings. I never sensed that they enjoyed them. I suspected that they considered going to church their civic duty. They put up with it. They did not like the loud and emotional responses from some in the congregation. Yet, they were friendly with everyone. My grandmother would often bring flowers to the services and visit those who were sick.

My grandparents were not comfortable with emotional displays. They could not comprehend the "holy rollers" who had come up from the South and would set up tents on vacant plots to dance and sing and be entranced by the Holy Spirit. Everyone I knew or associated with viewed the holy rollers as people who did not belong in our quiet community. To us, they were ridiculous. But they were also fascinating.

I compared notes about religious services with Tom, who went to another mostly middle-class church but was annoyed by the same things that annoyed me. We reinforced each other's views.

I wondered then and afterwards: What did my grandparents really think about religion? My grandfather never said a word about it within my hearing range. My grandmother was more openly religious. But it was not the religion of the church she regularly attended.

She never indicated that there was a conflict between the religious views that appealed to her and those of our local church which she felt obligated to attend. What appealed to her was the Unity Church and its teachings, a church headquartered not far away across the border in Missouri. She subscribed to Unity's magazine for kids, *Wee Wisdom*, to give to me to read. She listed to Unity's radio broadcasts. She occasionally attended Unity services at their temple in Kansas City, Missouri. She was pleased when in my last two years of high school I attended Unity services whenever I could instead of going to our local church. Unity was a "white" church that accepted our presence.

Since I felt some obligation to go to a church on Sunday, I was relieved to have an option. There was something congenial and peaceful about the Unity services. Its theology eluded me even though I listened carefully to the minister. No one wailed or moaned or even made any noise at all. The sermon was dry, without rhythm or poetry, but soothing. The singing was uplifting. There was no word of suffering. I felt comfortable there.

My grandmother was not the only one in my family attracted to Unity. Two of her sisters also went there. The son of one of them, two years older than I was, also attended. He and I looked so much alike that many could not tell us apart until I grew taller.

The difference between Unity and our local church provided me with a lot of nourishment for thought. It became clear to me that the differences were economic and about privilege and its lack. A favorite passage of the local minister was a quote from the Bible (my wording may not be accurate): "It is easier for a camel to go through the eye of a needle than for a rich man to enter the kingdom of God." It was honorable to be poor. It was honorable to suffer.

Not a word of this at Unity. It was a church of the upper middle class. Its message was to be loving and giving. They could afford to give. No one was suffering.

I found it curious that this "white" upper-middle-class church was much more appealing to me that our local "black" church. I attributed some of this to the fact that I was young and optimistic about my future. I was not willing to accept suffering. To treat suffering as honorable was to me another example of staying in your place and not striving to break free of the forces of racism.

But the bias of the "white" church also troubled me. Being loving and giving was easy for them. Could they possibly understand the real suffering of others?

I stopped attending both churches when I went to college.

THE AUTHOR AND HIS GRANDFATHER
(reprinted with the permission of the Kenneth Spencer Research Library,
The University of Kansas Libraries)

Chapter 3

Moving Smoothly (More or Less) from One Environment to Another

Going to college meant that I had to move from an all-"black" community to a predominately "white" one. I looked forward to it. I believed that my future depended on getting a good education and getting recognized for what I could do. I had no intention of living a segregated life.

I was mentally well-armed as I entered the University of Kansas. My father, my mother, and my aunt had all graduated from there. All three had Phi Beta Kappa keys in honor of their academic performances. They had excelled in competition with "white" classmates, so I knew I would too.

I knew that if there was prejudice there against "blacks," my parents and aunt had found a way to succeed in spite of it. They had already demonstrated to the University that "blacks" could be smarter than the average "white" and compete successfully with the best of them. I did not have to prove it again; they had already done so. They had helped pave the road that I could travel more easily than they had.

And before them, my grandfather had faced discrimination at the Indiana University but still received a bachelor's degree in physics. Due to racism, he was not allowed to reside on campus. A "white" family took him in. Clearly, looking "white" was to his advantage. Clearly too, there were "whites" who were willing to help, at least a little.

I also had had prior experiences with "whites" who treated me with respect. So I expected the same from my college teachers and classmates.

I had two "white" employers when I worked a few hours a week in high school, after I had given up on *The Call*. One was a veterinarian, a man who was socially inept and somewhat like the doctor in the "Doc Martin" television series, but unlike Doc Martin, he related to dogs better than to people. In spite of his ineptness, he treated me with respect within his gruff abilities. The other consisted of the owners and managers of three shoe stores in downtown Kansas City, Missouri. I was a lowly stock boy. They too treated me with respect. The "black" janitor who had worked for them for some time told me that they were good employers and that he liked working for them. I was told that both employers, the veterinarian and the shoe store owners, were Jews. I had no idea what a Jew was in those days. They were just "white" people to me.

My other experience was with people my own age. While in high school, I was a participant in a weeklong program called "Boys State." (It still exists.) Boys State involved electing students to be legislators, judges, and other officials to run a mock government. I think there was another "black" student there. This program went smoothly, and I saw no sign of "racial" prejudice. I was not looking for prejudice, since a schoolmate had gone the year before and told me that it was a lot of fun.

These positive experiences, along with my attendance at Unity, did not erase or diminish my awareness of racism. The lunch counters of Kansas City, Kansas were still segregated. It was in the summer of 1957, just before I was going off to college, that I decided to test the segregated system, motivated by my thirst on a hot summer day. On the main street downtown, I went into a pharmacy with mostly occupied seats at a food counter, sat down on an empty seat as the man next to me gave me a questioning look, and ordered a soft drink. The waitress behind the counter prepared the drink, handed it to me, and then said that I was not allowed to sit at the counter. I was very thirsty, so I moved to a merchandise counter and finished my drink.

This was a curious compromise. I got the drink and was allowed to consume it in the store but not at the counter. I wondered if the waitress thought this up on the spot. In a segregated system, I would have thought that I should have been denied service altogether. In any event, it was a compromise that left segregation intact while I quenched my thirst. The customers all looked the other way and said nothing.

A few years later, this particular component of segregation in the Kansas City area was abolished due to a series of demonstrations that my aunt helped to organize in Kansas City, Missouri.

(The distinction between Kansas City, Kansas, and Kansas City, Missouri, is important, not only because they are two different but adjacent cities, but also because Missouri entered the Union as a "slave" state in which slavery was legal. After some violent battles, Kansas entered the Union as a "free" state where slavery was not legal.[20] This legacy was apparent to me as a child. The "blacks" across the border in Missouri generally were not as well off as the "blacks" in Kansas, even though segregation was also the norm in Kansas. When I traveled as a child further from Kansas, eastward through Missouri to Virginia, "blacks" seemed far worse off in St. Louis than in Kansas City, Missouri.)

So I entered the university knowing from my experience at the counter that segregation was fully intact in my hometown. I assumed that it was also fully intact in the university town of Lawrence, forty miles away. I hoped that I would not see it on campus.

My first encounter when I arrived on campus was at the scholarship hall—a university-owned residence for above-average students— where I had been admitted. I received a friendly welcome and was directed to my room, a small room occupied by four students. The beds were in a dormitory. My roommates were friendly. I saw no signs of hostility from anyone. I did not like my cramped quarters, but at least we were all in the same boat.

Everyone was "white" except for me. "'White'-except-for-me" was my new norm. Although there were many "black" students on campus, usually I was the only "black" person in my classes, but Tom was there too in a few of my honors courses. He and I had parted ways a few years ago, but I was glad to see him in these classes.

I cannot say that there was no "racial" prejudice. I had made up my mind not to look for it. I knew that it is easy to misinterpret words and behavior to mean something different from what is intended. Unless prejudice was obvious, I would not assume that it was present. So if there was prejudice, I did not see it, except in the very few instances where it was obvious. I may have had blinders that preventing me from seeing non-obvious prejudice. On the other hand, perhaps it was not there to see.

My first encounter with possible prejudice was certainly subject to interpretation. I had taken entrance examinations given to those who had already been admitted, and I was assigned to a counselor to determine whether I belonged in the honors classes. I had scored in the upper-ninetieth percentile on the part of the test pertaining to mathematics, but only in the mid-sixtieth percentile on the part of the test pertaining to language. My counselor had no doubt that I belonged in honors classes in mathematics but not in English. But there were two honors classes in mathematics, a regular honors and a high honors. The counselor said that I scored one point below the threshold for getting into the high honors class. (As I recall, the threshold was fifty-two points, and I had scored fifty-one.) But he said that he would put me in the high honors class anyway because, he intimated, I probably did not have the best mathematics teachers in high school, so my score was high given my circumstances. I felt a desire to protest and not accept something that I did not deserve and might not be qualified for. But then I also thought that maybe he had a point, that maybe others had had better instruction in mathematics than I had. I almost told him that I thought my math teachers were quite good, but I had no way to compare them with those in some of the more privileged high schools. I thought that probably his view of my high school was biased, a result of prejudice. But he was acting in my favor. I accepted his good intentions and kept quiet.

So the counselor was engaged in an individual act of affirmative action long before anyone knew anything about it. His prejudice was to assume that I had had poor schooling, so that I was probably more capable than my test scores showed. It was a form of prejudice used in my support. So I entered the high honors mathematics class knowing that I had scored at least a point lower than everyone else but determined to prove that I belonged there. For three semesters I had a wonderful teacher, Dr. G. Baley Price, and I gradually worked my way up to join those at the top of the class.

My decision not to look for "racial" prejudice and to be generous in how I interpreted others' words and behavior served me well. I was upset when my first paper in English, a required course for everyone, received a C-. How could this be? (This was before the grade inflation which began after I finished graduate school.) I discretely looked around wondering what grade others got, but they were not exposing their grades. Then the most articulate member of the class spoke up to ask tactfully whether the teacher was being especially strict on this first paper. He too had received a grade much lower than what he had expected. I felt relieved. The teacher wanted us all to do better. I concluded that he had no "racial" bias. I also knew that I had scored only around the sixty-fifth percentile on the language part of my entrance exam, and that I needed to improve. As I improved, so did my grades. I had no doubt that the teacher was being fair to all.

But a classmate from high school was in the same English class. When she got a D on one of her papers, she assumed that the teacher was "racially" biased. I was convinced by then that she had made the wrong assumption. She was light-skinned, and it's even possible the teacher did not know that she was "black." The problem with her assumption is that it created oppression where it did not exist. Instead of working to improve, she had imposed on herself a reason for her low grade over which she had no control. That meant that there was no point in trying to improve. The assumption of racism was self-defeating.

I might have been offended by a comment made by my physics teacher, but I was not. Tom was in this honors class too, and the teacher got us confused when he was handing back graded tests. He said something about getting us confused and laughed. Tom did not look like me, but we had the same skin color. His comment called attention to our being the only two "blacks" in the class. I knew by then that the teacher was fair-minded, so I was amused by his comment. I remembered that he was supportive, not offended or embarrassed, when I showed in class a simpler way to solve a problem that he had just solved on the blackboard. I also thought about how many times I could not tell one "white" person from another.

Only once did I clearly experience racism from a classmate. I had just given a talk in speech class, and the teacher offered praise. But a woman in front of the class said, "Yes, it was good, *for him*." She repeated and emphasized "for him." It was clear what she meant. The teacher reaffirmed his praise, omitting "for him." I did not feel that his response was adequate, but nothing more was said. One student gave the woman a disapproving look. The others were mute.

My only other clear experience with racism occurred off campus, in town. The waiters at the eating places right next to campus paid no attention when I entered or ordered. They treated me like everyone else. But one evening I went with two of my housemates farther into town and sat down in a restaurant. The waiter said that they did not serve "Negroes," but the other two could order. The other two were disgusted and did not order. One of them, philosopher Kenneth Megill, who was one of my three roommates, became a lifelong friend.

My two companions suggested that we go somewhere else, a place that had food and dancing. It was not near the campus. As we walked in after paying a modest entry fee, thus indicating that we had been admitted, one woman sitting at a table gave me a glare. She was the same person who had made the insulting comment in the speech class. I gave her a glance, satisfied in some respect that, by being there, I had gotten even.

Fear of racism had an effect. I had heard from other "black" students that the barbershops near campus would not cut their hair. For my first few haircuts, I walked some distance to the "black" area of town for my haircuts. After several months, I decided that this was a waste of time, so I walked into the barbershop next to campus. I was seated, my hair was cut, and nothing was said. That barbershop had me as a new customer after that.

Fear of racism had another more serious effect. I decided that I would not date a "white" student. I thought that the stress of breaking that perceived barrier would be more than I could handle. I was there to succeed academically, and that required a certain degree of emotional isolation. That decision did not change until after my second year of graduate school.

That decision, of course, led to a degree of loneliness. Towards the end of my sophomore year, I wondered if the solution was to abandon my "white" home environment and join one of the "black" fraternities where access to "black" women would be part of my environment. Many, perhaps most, "black" students, men and women, made the choice to live in a "black" environment. The fraternities and sororities were segregated. I decided to visit one of "black" fraternities to explore this option.

I knew which of the two main "black" fraternities would be more congenial. I called to let them know I was coming. They arranged for me to come to dinner and stay overnight.

The fraternity's home was mostly empty when I arrived in the late afternoon. A couple of the residents introduced themselves, and after some awkward moments, one offered to show me around. In the basement was a recreational area that included a ping-pong table. The resident wondered if I would play. I agreed, and after a few games it was clear that we were mismatched. I was by far the better player. He said that he would arrange for me to play the best ping-pong player in the fraternity. An hour or so later, that match occurred, and again I was clearly the better player.

This contest was symbolic to me of an issue I had to face. In my scholarship hall, I was at best only an average ping-pong player. In the fraternity, I would be the best. If I stayed where I was, I could be continually challenged to become a better player. In the fraternity, there would be no challenge.

Academically it was the same issue, as I realized from my overnight stay. I heard students complaining about the racism of teachers, describing events that were subject to more generous interpretations. The claim of racism, like that of the other "black" student in my English class, was an easy way to excuse sub-par performances. It was a way to avoid an academic challenge to improve.

In my scholarship hall, I was surrounded by people who strived to improve. Many of them were honors students. We challenged each other. Ken and I took a philosophy course together. I remember one evening that we struggled together to unravel the grammar of Thomas Hobbes. Another of my housemates was a classmate in the physics class, and we had many discussions about how to solve the problems assigned to the class. Many evenings I would join some of my housemates in friendly but persistent probes of the Catholicism of two others, who always had answers that seemed to take us around in impenetrable circles. We'd listen to Beethoven through a Heathkit amplifier, and I would construct my own stereo system which I tried to make better than the one next door. Everywhere there were challenges, new ideas and new awareness that broadened my perspective.

I concluded that at the fraternity, I would be academically at the top, just as I was at ping-pong. It would be a challenge there for me to motivate the others to succeed and combat the self-negating culture they were creating. At the scholarship hall I was among academic peers and would be continually challenged and grow.

I decided to give the fraternity idea one more chance in the hope of eventually obtaining something approaching intimate female contact. I was invited to a party sponsored by the fraternity and a "black" sorority, the kind of event I had been missing. I went and felt like a fish out of water. I realized that what I wanted was a female companion who was an academic equal—like the woman my father had succeeded in finding. If such a woman existed among the "black" women on campus when I was there, I did not meet her. But I also did not make much of an effort to find her.

So I continued my "white"-except-for-me life and decided that solving the lack of female companionship would have to wait. That made sense, since I intended to go to graduate school and not get married until much later. The sorority women were looking for husbands.

Overall I had numerous experiences where I thought I would encounter racism but did not. I sensed, but did not confirm until later, that racism would have been more evident if my skin had been darker. Later I heard stories from dark-skinned "blacks" that shocked me. They told of blatant racist occurrences that I had never experienced. That made it clear to me that the relative lack of racism that I experienced personally was not an accurate indicator of the extent to which racism existed.

I returned to the scholarship hall for my fifth semester. For the sixth semester, Ken invited me to join him and another housemate to live off campus. I hoped we would not be defeated by housing discrimination, but I agreed. Our landlord had no problem with my presence. Ken and I lived there for the remaining three semesters; our third roommate left prior to our senior years.

In the summer before my senior year, I worked under Ken's brother at the National Bureau of Standards in Boulder, Colorado. Boulder provided me with a refreshing contrast to Lawrence. The segregation that was prevalent in Lawrence was not present in Boulder. When I returned to K.U. for my senior year, I wrote an article comparing Boulder to Lawrence, obviously favoring Boulder. The article was published as the lead editorial in the K.U. campus newspaper. That the paper chose to publish my article revealed to me that I had support on campus for my views beyond my friends and professors.

I did learn of the racism—and sexism—of a well-known visiting European philosophy professor from whom I had taken two courses and received A's. I learned from Ken that at a small gathering honoring the visitor, which I did not attend, the professor had proclaimed that philosophy was for "white men" and that others did not have the mentality for it. At the same gathering, the professor commented on the final exams in one of his courses and said that someone named Hodge, whom he could not remember, had written the best exam. Ken was amused when he told me, indicating that the professor had unknowingly refuted himself.

I began college intending to major in engineering physics. But by our senior years, Ken and I had in common our desires to go to graduate school to get PhDs in philosophy. We were inspired by three K.U. philosophy professors who had recently received PhDs from Yale: Peter Caws, Richard T. DeGeorge, and Charles Landesman. With their support, Ken and I were both admitted to Yale Graduate School. I was also aided by a Danforth Fellowship that covered four years. Ken received an award to be an exchange student and went to Germany for a year, then he came to Yale when I was beginning my second year.

We had both succeeded in our quests and both received our PhDs from Yale, but by different routes.

Graduate school for me was about much more than academics. It was also a time to reflect and decide how to live in the world.

It was the early to mid-1960s. The civil rights movement was gaining steam. A war was escalating in Vietnam. A president was assassinated. Malcolm X was beginning to make sense once he decided that "white" people were not the enemy. Betty Friedan published *The Feminine Mystique* which I read not long after it was published. I was beginning to see war, racism and sexism as somehow linked.

How was any of this related to philosophy? I was a sophomore when I took my first philosophy course from Peter Caws. Ken encouraged me to take that class. I was captivated by what I was reading. Here were people grappling with what it means to know, what is real and not real. By then I already knew that what people thought was true about "race" was false. If that was false, what else was false? Here, in the philosophy class, people were facing this directly and looking for the right way to find the truth. This was what I wanted to study!

By the end of the course, however, I had concluded that something was wrong with what I was reading. Philosophers had taken a wrong turn in trying to answer the right questions. I decided that I would keep studying philosophy until I figured out what had gone wrong, and, hopefully, offer a way to correct it. I sensed then that there was a connection between errors in ways of thinking and social ills.

My studies thereafter were bifurcated. There was the philosophy I studied in the classroom. But just as influential, if not more so, was the philosophy I read outside the classroom: John Paul Sartre, Albert Camus, Gabriel Marcel, Erich Fromm (in my view an important philosopher as well as a psychologist), and many others. These were writers connecting philosophy to social issues, many of whom were confronting the mentality of fascism and Nazism through which they had lived or from which they had escaped.

What they were confronting was the same mentality that produced racism in America. The problems of Europe and those of America were linked. These were the issues that excited me.

In this background, John Dewey's philosophy began to make sense. Dewey was a social reformer and philosophy was an integral part of his reforms. But there was more to his thinking than what appeared on the surface. I became intrigued with his intellectual predecessor, Charles Saunders Peirce, who became the primary focus of the two dissertations I wrote. (I wrote two, because the first one was not accepted.)

With overcoming racism an underlying motive, my studies and my personal life were interlinked.

During my graduate studies, my personal life took several leaps forward.

One critical leap was entirely mental. I was an "aha" moment that changed the way I saw myself in relation to my social surroundings.

Prior to that moment, I had lived to be an example to others of why "racial" prejudice made no sense. In my mind I was saying to others, "This is me. How could you be prejudiced against me?" In other words: Look, I am a nice guy who is as intelligent as you are (if not more so). This, of course, was mostly unconscious. I suspect I picked it up from my family.

My "aha" was, first, to realize that I was doing this, and second, to realize that this way of living was a reaction to racism. Since racism is nonsensical, I was living in reaction to something that was nonsensical. That meant that this way of living was nonsensical.

Thus, I had to be myself, not a reaction to something that made no sense.

As I recall, this moment stopped me in my tracks as I walked along one of the streets that goes through the Yale campus. I repeatedly went over these new thoughts for a few minutes before continuing my walk. I felt a great weight lifted from my shoulders. I did not have to prove anything to anybody. I was free to be me.

As a person freed from this burden, I was able to break out of my self-imposed cocoon. I realized that my mental health required that I connect more to others. I spent two summers in Quaker-sponsored programs where those connections began to occur. When the first of these summers began, I was still seeing myself as in a "white"-except-for-me world. The connections that occurred subsequently were both socially relevant and personally satisfying. They also changed how I saw myself in the world.

As I met new people during these summers, I could see how much I was attracted to intelligent, strong women. I received enough encouragement from them to overcome my shyness, and friendships and loves followed. These connections are probably partly why I was attracted to *The Feminine Mystique*, Simon de Beauvoir's *The Second Sex,* and other feminist writings. I began to see a connection between racism and the oppression of women. I began to identify the way of thinking that led to both.[21]

Seeing this connection was not just a mental process. I was enjoying friendships with women who also sensed that we were politically aligned in fighting a common oppression that affected us. We were also opposed to the American aggression in Vietnam. Somehow we knew these things were linked—the war, racism and sexism—even though we could not articulate the linkage. There was this bigger social and political context connecting us to one another beyond the fact that we just liked each other.

My "white"-except-for-me world dissipated into "us." "Us," however, was not everyone. We were women and men with shared values, values that were feminist, anti-racist, and anti-war, and that subsequently included support for gay rights.

During this time and lasting into the present, I have never forgotten a dark-skinned classmate that I had been friendly with as a child. I admired his intelligence. He was the best speller in a class that contained some very intelligent classmates. He told me of instances when his mother physically abused him. He and his mother lived in poverty. At some point, I believe it was in the ninth grade, he stopped coming to school. I heard that his mother had decided to return to a southern home and, of course, had taken her son with her. I have worried ever since that his intelligence would not be rewarded, that his poverty would defeat him, and that he would not thrive in a southern racist environment that was worse than the one he had left.

Our society deprives people like him of the reasonable opportunity to live fulfilling lives and contribute to the well-being of others. A few overcome the socially and politically created obstacles placed in their paths. Most do not.

PART II

CROSS-GROUP INTIMACIES

Chapter 4

Intimacies in Early America

By the time modern Europeans landed on the American continents at the end of the fifteenth century, the descendants of the first Americans, the indigenous peoples of America ("Indians," "Native Americans"),[22] occupied the Western hemisphere above and below the equator. Beginning in the fifteenth century, modern Europeans arrived in large numbers and encountered a variety of existing settlements, some warlike and hostile, some peaceful and friendly, some with sophisticated governing structures. The relationships between the new Europeans and the existing occupants were complex, ranging from brutal attacks to love and marriage.

The first modern Europeans who established lasting settlements in the Americas were Spaniards who had landed in the Caribbean and Mexico and spread west, south and north into what is now Florida, Texas and California. Portuguese landed in Brazil and spread north, west and south. Arrivals from France entered North America by way of the Saint Lawrence River and traveled into the interior and all the way down the Mississippi River to Louisiana. Arrivals from England, Ireland and Holland came later, followed by arrivals from Germany and many other European countries from the east and Russia from the west through Alaska. Over time and into the nineteenth century and following, England became the dominant but not exclusive colonial force in North America.[23]

The United States had completely freed itself from England's control by 1783, but the continued dominant influence of England is obvious. English is the primary language. The legal system, with a few exceptions, was inherited from England.[24] The concept of human rights—a concept by no means exclusively English—emerged in England in the Magna Carta of 1215. Even today, this document makes Chinese authorities uneasy.[25] The concept of rights contained in it evolved into the Bill of Rights in the U.S. Constitution, almost six centuries later.[26] The Magna Carta itself was a development from England's Charter of Liberties written in 1100, a document that affirmed that the power of the King was not unlimited.[27]

Thus, the behavior and attitudes of the English in England towards Africans and indigenous people in America is relevant to understanding their early and subsequent treatment of these people in North America. There were similarities as well as remarkable differences in the way the English regarded these people in the two countries.

Black, White and Tan

In 1555 John Lok (not to be confused with the famous philosopher John Locke, 1632-1704) brought five sub-Saharan West Africans to England to teach them enough so that they could help facilitate trade between England and West Africa. The five went voluntarily.[28] Lok's act presupposed that the Africans did, in fact, have the capability to learn what was necessary and would voluntarily and peacefully act as intermediaries between England and West Africa.

There is no hint here that Africans should be enslaved or treated as inferior. Lok must have assumed that the Africans would be sufficiently accepted in England to enable him to accomplish his purpose. His act also presupposed that existing trade between England and West Africa in goods such as gold, pepper and ivory would continue and expand.[29] Such trade had begun with the voyages of William Hawkins in 1530.[30]

But Englishmen did not all think alike. Even much more so than today, the England of Lok's time was divided socially, religiously and politically. In today's American terms, we might say the primary division was between conservatives and liberals. It was a hostile division. A century after Lok's venture, the political and religious divisions in England became so volatile that they led to a civil war—where the first did not have the good fortune of becoming last because their heads were chopped off.[31] That war did not settle matters and additional vicious internal battles followed.[32]

Thus, we cannot talk about "the English" as though they were of one mind.

It seems to be a common error of historians, journalists, and common folk to attribute to a whole society the characteristics of a dominant group, whether the dominant group is a majority or a controlling minority. Every large society has its conservatives and liberals, those who oppress and those who oppose oppression, those who wish to impose hierarchical order and those who favor egalitarianism, those who fit in and those who do not. The dissidents and the powerless are often ignored for their contributions, even though, through their influence, they may become dominant in another era.

Lok and the Englishman John Hawkins did not think alike. Nor did John Hawkins think like his father, William. A few years after Lok's mission, John Hawkins went to West Africa to capture or otherwise obtain Africans to sell at a profit to Spanish settlers.[33] To John Hawkins, Africans were not people with whom to trade as equals but a source of human capital to be sold to those who wanted them for slaves.[34] Some others, following in Hawkins' footsteps, brought captured Africans to England, resulting in a significant African presence by 1600, especially in London and some other English port cities.[35] In the eighteenth century, many Africans and those of partial African descent came to England as slaves or servants of English landowners and government officials who had returned to England from the West Indies. Some came later as freed men who had served on the British side in the American Revolutionary War.[36]

While some Americans might regard as traitors those "blacks" who fought with the British, they too were fighting for their freedom—freedom from slavery and oppression. It was a rational choice. The famous 1772 *Somerset's Case*[37] had the predictable and eventual effect of abolishing slavery in England. This case was decided before the

American war of independence and nearly a century before slavery ended throughout the United States.

Prior to the *Somerset's Case*, Africans' legal status in England was not clear, and jurists debated whether they could be considered property.[38] Most of them did menial labor and perhaps many were regarded as indentured servants and treated similarly to English indentured servants (sometimes well, sometimes not).[39] By 1764, about 3 percent of London's population was of African origin.[40] There was widespread discrimination against them, and many were treated as or considered to be slaves.[41]

Not all those of African descent in England were treated poorly. One of them—for example, Francis Barber, born into slavery in Jamaica—was brought to England by his master, sent to school and freed by his master's will. In 1752, Mr. Barber became a trusted servant and friend to the famous writer and critic, Dr. Samuel Johnson, and stayed in that capacity, with a couple of short absences, until Dr. Johnson's death in 1784. Dr. Johnson arranged for Mr. Barber's further education and in his will left Mr. Barber a generous life-long income and a gold watch. Some of the descendants of Mr. Barber and his English wife still live in England.[42]

Dr. Johnson was not alone in having a servant of African descent, as such servants were at times considered fashionable in upper-class English households, which usually treated them well and provided for their education. In the eighteenth century, the English lower class often treated the mostly male African descendants as of their own class, including marrying them. An English marriage of a black-skinned African man to an English woman was recorded as early as 1578,[43] and there were probably others. Some strenuously objected to the new hues added to the population; others had no problem with it and some contributed to it. In recognizing the equal humanity of the Africans, the lower-class English who married Africans, and the neighbors who accepted them, contributed positively to English history.[44]

Thus, color prejudice varied in England: for some it was quite strong, for some it was absent, for some it was mixed with or replaced by religious prejudice against those who were not Christianized; but, on the other hand, many did not take religion very seriously. In other words, though racism was clearly present, there was no uniformity among the English in their attitudes towards darker-skinned people. It is historically significant that the official racism and legalized segregation that developed in America did not reach such extremes in England.[45]

Given England's mixture of attitudes and treatment of Africans in their midst, it was not inevitable that America would become a land of entrenched slavery that ended only after an incredibly brutal Civil War, followed later by Jim Crow laws that made the southern United States a legal apartheid and the northern United States a segregated semi-apartheid until laws changed in the latter half of the twentieth century. In spite of this history of slavery and segregation, the efforts in America to fully separate the Africans from the English and other Europeans was not successful.

The cross-Atlantic slave trade did not begin with England. This slave trade was well underway before William Hawkins' venture in 1530. William Hawkins was looking to trade with Africans, not take slaves from them. Portugal and Spain were the European pioneers of this slave trade, which was well established by the end of the previous century.[46] Yet, many English contributed to this trade, both in England and in the new English colonies in America.

The first English settlement in the land now called the United States was on Roanoke Island (North Carolina) in 1587. That settlement disappeared for reasons not known.[47] The first lasting settlement occurred at Jamestown (Virginia) in 1607.[48] These settlements did not consist of high-minded Puritans looking for religious freedom, but merchants and adventurers authorized by Queen Elizabeth and King James to establish colonies in America.[49] Having slaves in America at that time was far from their minds.[50] West Africans had not yet arrived, and the earliest colonizers did not attempt until later to enslave the indigenous peoples.[51]

The first recorded lasting presence of West Africans in English America placed them in Virginia in 1619.[52] West African slaves of Portuguese and Spaniards were brought to the Americas a hundred years before then.[53] There is evidence that free people of African descent, notably Pedro Alonzo Nino, came to America as key members of Christopher Columbus' crew in 1492.[54] The status of these Africans is not known.[55] It was not until nearly twenty years later that some enslavement became evident, and it was not until after 1660 that slavery became a legal status in some of the colonies.[56] By 1700 slavery was firmly established.[57] But not all Africans were enslaved; some owned property, and some even owned slaves.[58]

By 1700 a new, disturbing problem was quite visible. There were now people whose ancestry was both African and English. These mixtures raised new questions about who was "black" and who was "white."[59]

Sex between Africans and English could not be hidden once the offspring emerged. How much was due to coercion and how much due to mutual cooperation cannot be determined, but cooperative sex clearly occurred and included marriages. Many of these cooperative relationships involved African men and English women.[60]

One of the documents revealing these early cooperative intimacies was a Maryland law enacted in 1664 addressing them: "An act concerning Negroes and other slaves." This Act specifically targeted English women who, "to the disgrace of our nation," married "Negro slaves." The Act provided that the wives of any future such marriages shall be slaves like the husbands, and that the issue of any such marriages *existing prior to this legislation* shall serve the husbands' master until they are thirty years of age, but no longer. This Act, thus, did not punish the "black" slaves in such marriages but punished the slaves' "white" wives by reducing their status.[61]

This was legislation of "whites" in power against powerless "whites," specifically, of the politically powerful "white" males who controlled legislation against powerless "white" women and their children. The heated language of the Act suggests that sexual jealousy was at work.

Two years before this Maryland enactment, Virginia enacted a law that doubled the fine for "fornication" between any Christian and a "negro man or woman."[62] Obviously such a law would not have been necessary if such "fornication" had not occurred. The 1664 Maryland Act apparently was not effective enough. A 1681 Maryland Act specifically attacked the "Lascivious and Lustful desires" of white women who married "Negroes."[63] Similarly, the 1662 Virginia act against fornication was apparently not very effective, for in 1691 Virginia had outlawed sex between "whites" and "blacks."[64] In addition, it punished any "white" woman who had a child by a "black" man, again focusing on the woman for punishment.[65]

These laws and similar laws in other colonies did not achieve their objective. Banning sex did not work.

In New England, as in the South, sex between "whites" and "blacks," whether slave or free, was common.[66] As early as 1663, evidence in a Massachusetts court made it apparent that a "white" man was the father of the child of another "white" man's slave.[67] "Ridicule, fines, divorce, and corporal punishment failed to stop the interbreeding of Negroes and whites."[68] The evidence appeared in the features of the resulting children.[69]

As Maryland's laws had done earlier, Massachusetts' laws in 1705-06 targeted sex between "Negro" men and "white" women, providing corporal punishment for both parties and requiring the "white" woman to care for the resulting children. The Massachusetts laws provided that sex between "white" men and "Negro" women was similarly punished,[70] but this kind of sex was rarely prosecuted.[71] However, the law did not affect existing marriages.[72] The result of such laws may have been to make marriages between "blacks" (whether free or slave) and indigenous Americans more common, for there was no legal barrier to them.[73] Other New England colonies did not pass such laws.[74]

In general, slavery in New England often involved close daily contact between masters and slaves in the masters' households. In some instances the relationships were congenial, and the slaves ate meals with and at the same table as the masters.[75] It would not be surprising if such close contact sometimes escalated to cooperative sex. In New England as elsewhere in the seventeenth and eighteenth centuries, marriages between "whites" and "blacks" did occur.[76]

It is often believed that most sex between "whites" and "blacks" during these times was forced by "white" men on slave women. There is plenty of irrefutable evidence that this frequently occurred, though it is not clear that mutual affection was entirely absent in every such case between master and slave.[77] There is also plenty of evidence of cooperative "white"-"black" sexual relationships, both inside and outside of marriage, involving both "white" men and "white" women with "black" partners.[78] In the 1750s, Massachusetts' court records show divorces granted to "white" men because their "white" wives had had sex with "blacks" that resulted in children.[79] In 1759, nearly one hundred years after Maryland law first attacked marriages between "white" women and slaves, a Maryland man placed an advertisement in a newspaper renouncing responsibility for his wife's debts, because, the advertisement states, his wife had slept with her "Negro" slave and had a child by him. The man's anger in the ad was directed at his wife, not at the slave.[80]

In the eighteenth century, cooperative sex between "whites" and "blacks" was quite visible in Charleston, South Carolina, mostly between "white" men and "black" women, but also in North Carolina where a visitor noted that it was "white" women who took charge.[81] During the 1770's, in Charleston, "black" women held dances and invited "white" men who attended.[82] It is unlikely that these dances were purely about dancing. In New Orleans, it was common practice for a "white" man to take in a "colored" female companion and for them to raise their children. [83] "New Orleans was notorious for the extent of 'race mixing' that went on there, but it was common in other Southern communities as well."[84]

As early as 1666, the term "mulatto" began to appear in Virginia records.[85] In 1679, reference to a "mulatto" slave appeared in Massachusetts court records.[86] In the late seventeenth and early eighteenth centuries, New England laws incorporated the term "mulatto" (variously spelled) and often lumped "Negroes" and "mulattoes" together.[87] By lumping them together, "mulattoes"—the children of "white"-"black" unions—began to be treated like "Negroes"—though often exceptions were made for those who looked "white." Since "mulattoes" sometimes married those called "Indians," and "half-breed" "Indians" married "blacks" and "mulattoes," the result was children of English, "Indian," and African ancestry.[88] In the Carolinas and Georgia, another term was often used: "mustee." That was the term for "black"-"Indian" and "white"-"Indian" mixtures.[89] "Mustees," "Mulattoes," and "Negroes" were often treated similarly.[90]

As I observed as a child (Chapter 1), as I have observed subsequently, and as we know from the workings of genetics, the skins of the children of a couple where one member of the couple is dark-skinned and the other is light-skinned can range from dark to light. The children's skin color may even be darker than that of the darkest parent or lighter than that of the lightest parent due to prior ancestry. Even twins can have remarkably different skin color. In some cases, some of the children of such couples can look "white" even if one or both parents does not look "white." Thus, the line drawn between who is "white" and who is "black" is a matter of historical curiosity, especially when a person who appears to be "black" and another person who appears to be "white" are the children of the same parents. How were these lines drawn?

In many cases the lines were drawn on the basis of appearance, not on actual ancestry. "What the matter came down to, of course, was visibility."[91]

A documented case in the 1730s involved Gideon Gibson and his sons, all of whom married "white" women. Mr. Gibson was known to have had "Negro" ancestry, therefore, according to custom, he was a "Negro." Yet, because he was free, and because his father was free, the Governor of South Carolina declared that he and his sons would remain free. Thereafter, Gibson and his sons were regarded by most as "white."[92] A Charleston merchant, while in England, noted that Gibson and his sons looked more "white" than many distinguished Englishmen who were descendants of French refugees.[93]

It is not known how many people of European-African ancestry became "white," since this process of "passing" was often done with the secretiveness required for its success.[94] But, beginning with the first free offspring of marriages between European women and African men in the seventeenth century, people in the colonies migrated from "black" to "white."[95] By the nineteenth and twentieth centuries, "This migration from black to white had been happening for centuries and continued to occur on a daily basis."[96] As a consequence of "passing," many today who think they are purely "white" have African ancestry, not counting the Europeans who had African ancestry before they arrived in America (See Chapters 5 and 6.)

Not all "white"-looking "blacks" became "white." My grandfather was an example of that. W. E. B. DuBois, while he was attending Harvard in the late nineteenth century, noted that two women to whom he was attracted were "Negro" but looked "white." One of them succeeded in graduating from Vassar—which then, in the late nineteenth century, did not accept "Negroes"—before Vassar discovered that she was a "Negro" due to her ancestry. DuBois defended her deception.[97]

The story of America's mixtures is illustrated by the Hemings family. (See the chart of family relationships on the facing page.) Sally Hemings' maternal grandfather was an English captain whose vessel traveled between England and Virginia. Her maternal grandmother was a slave from Africa living in Virginia. Their child was Elizabeth Hemings, born into slavery. The Englishman reportedly wanted the child, but the child's owner would not agree. The child took the Englishman's last name: Hemings. Sally's grandmother's subsequent master ("white") had children with his wife ("white"), one of whom was named Martha. After the master's wife died, he had several children with Elizabeth, his slave. Sally was one of these children. Sally, as the child of the master's slave, was also the master's slave, but when the master died, her ownership passed to Martha, who was Sally's half sister. Martha married Thomas Jefferson, who would later become president of the United States. They had two surviving children. Martha then died. Due to Martha's marriage to Jefferson, Jefferson owned Sally.

Sally and Jefferson had four surviving children, all with her surname. One of them, a son named Beverly, lived as a "white" person, married a "white" woman and had children. Another of them, a daughter named Harriet, married a "white" man and had children who, like Beverly's children, were considered "white." A second son married a woman of African or mixed descent. The third son, Madison (who explained these relationships[98]), married Mary McCoy. Mary's maternal grandmother was a slave, and her maternal grandfather was the grandmother's "white" master who later freed the grandmother. Madison and Mary had eight surviving children, five of whom married and also had children.[99]

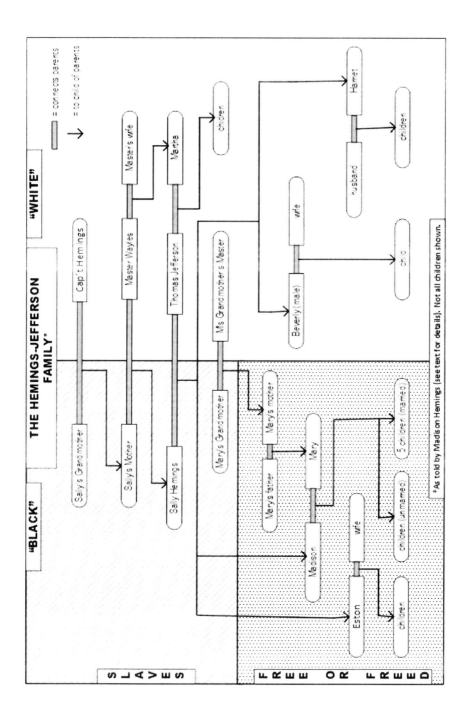

THE HEMINGS–JEFFERSON FAMILY*

"BLACK"   "WHITE"

= connects parents
→ = to child of parents

S
L
A
V
E
S

F
R
E
E   O R
F
R
E
E
D

Cap't Hemings
Sally's Grandmother

Master Wayles   Master's wife
Sally's Mother

Thomas Jefferson   Martha
Sally Hemings   children

My Grandmother's Master
Mary's Grandmother

Harriet   "husband"
children

Beverly (male)   wife
child

Mary's mother
Mary's father   Mary
Madison   5 children (married)
children (unmarried)
wife   Eston
children

*As told by Madison Hemings (see text for details). Not all children shown.

Here in a nutshell is a revelation of the absurdity of "racial" distinctions in America. Two children of Sally and Jefferson were "black"; the other two were "white." The "black" children and the "white" children had the same parents.

It appears that some of these master-slave relationships were a matter of mutual consent. Madison Hemings described his father, Thomas Jefferson, as "uniformly kind to all about him."[100] Madison and his siblings became free when they were adults, apparently under an agreement between Jefferson and Sally.[101] Such an agreement indicates that Jefferson and Sally had a cooperative relationship. According to Madison, Sally knew that she had the choice of remaining free in France when she accompanied Jefferson to Paris, so it was her choice to remain with Jefferson after they came to an agreement. Given the status of married women at the time, the difference between being married and being a voluntary slave mistress whose children would be freed might not have been great. Perhaps a similar liaison led Mary McCoy's grandfather to free her grandmother.

The only thing that was unusual about the Hemings family was that Thomas Jefferson was involved. The family illustrates the intimacies that often occurred between masters and slaves. As with Sally Hemings and Jefferson, some of these intimacies were congenial, especially when the slaves may have been family members or related by marriage.

The story of the Heming's family is detailed in Annette Gordon-Reed's *The Hemingses of Monticello*.[102]

The outcome of such intimacies, whether congenial or coerced, was obvious to Frederick Douglass. In his first autobiography, published in 1845, he states, "[I]t is nevertheless plain that a very different-looking class of people are springing up at the south, and are now held in slavery, from those originally brought to this country from Africa."[103] He was himself a former slave who escaped to freedom. He noted that thousands were like him in having a "white" father.[104] What he observed was part of the outcome of what had been going on for over two centuries and continued afterward.

In view of these intimacies, we must conclude that the passions that led to the Civil War was about more than politics and economics. The visceral emotional attachment to the "southern way of life" was as much about the sexual privileges of the ruling land-owning class as about economics.

Red, White and Tan

The concept of religious freedom in America may not have developed without the help of some indigenous Americans. The primary source of that concept in the American colonies was Roger Williams. Williams survived because some indigenous Americans assisted him in his escape on foot in 1634, in the dead of winter, from the intolerant Massachusetts Bay Colony that was seeking to capture him and send him back to an unwelcoming England, or worse. Williams' survival would have been unlikely without this assistance. Some of these "Indians" provided shelter than enabled Williams to survive the winter.[105]

With their help, he made it to what is now Rhode Island. There, he established a freer and tolerant community that he called "Providence." In 1644 Providence officially established freedom of religion and the separation of church and state—apparently for the first time in the European world and possibly for the first time in recorded history.[106] In 1647 that freedom expanded to the rest of Rhode Island, which became the only place in the colonies where such freedom existed.[107] In keeping with this new concept of freedom, in 1652 Rhode Island became the first colony to outlaw slavery.[108] (Unfortunately, this wonderful legacy was desecrated in the following century when Providence became a major center of the slave trade.)[109]

Why was Roger Williams aided by the indigenous Americans during his escape? It was because he related to them differently from most of the other colonists. He treated them as equals, traded with them, socialized with them, and learned their language. In return, they respected him.[110]

His different relationships with them partially stemmed from English common law, with which Williams was well-versed due to his close relationship with the renowned English jurist Edward Coke. In Williams' view of the common law, the indigenous Americans owned the land, and the English king was wrong to think that he could designate any of the new world's soil as belonging to the English. According to Williams, if the English wanted any of this land, they would have to purchase it from the indigenous Americans or at least get their permission.[111] Since the colonists did not get that permission, they were illegal intruders.

Consistent with his views, Williams obtained permission from the Narragansetts to establish Providence. They agreed on its boundaries.[112] That agreement allowed the experiment with freedom of religion to flourish, an experiment that would change the course of American and Western history.

As we know, the long-term relationships between the European intruders and the indigenous people of America did not turn out well. It did not have to be that way. In relating to the indigenous peoples, the intruders could have followed the example of Roger Williams, but the dominant ruling powers among them did not.

The dominant ruling powers among the early Puritans punished or exiled those who offended them. Although the Puritans made a notable and often overlooked advance towards democracy by establishing in 1641 "The Massachusetts Body of Liberties," the 94th listed law in this Body called for the death of anyone who "shall have or worship any other god, but the lord god," along with death for blasphemy, adultery or gay male sex.

Among the exiled was Thomas Morton, who was not a Puritan and had arrived separately in 1624 from England as part of a small commercially oriented group. Morton had come not to steal the lands of the indigenous peoples but to trade with them, which he did successfully. He also socialized with them and danced and slept with the women. He was so open about it that, with his sense of humor, he called his small settlement "Merrymount" and raised an 80-foot Maypole. To the Puritans, he was a licentious heathen who consorted with the savages. He so offended the Puritan rulers that they captured him and sent him back to England. When Morton returned after his first exile, the Puritan rulers imprisoned him, exiled him again (but spared his life), and burned Merrymount to the ground.[113]

Thus, the early conflict between the English intruders and the indigenous population was also a conflict of the English against the English, of the English who wanted to dominate the indigenous peoples and those who wanted to relate to them with respect and as equals. The indigenous peoples respected the latter and abhorred the former. Their respect for the latter included their frequent acceptance of marriages between them and the newcomers.

The usually told stories of the relationship of the indigenous to the intruders are dominated by conflict which continues to this day.[114] But there was also cooperative sex, love and marriage.

We were taught in grade school about the marriage of the indigenous "Indian" princess Pocahontas (daughter of the Chief of the Powhatans) to John Rolfe, which occurred in 1614. (The details of her much-publicized prior relationship with Captain John Smith are in doubt.) There are a multitude of living descendants of their child, Thomas Rolfe. These descendants merged seamlessly into the "white" population.[115] The mixture of indigenous peoples and the English in America may have begun there, but it cannot be ruled out that such mixtures occurred prior to that, without marriage or recorded marriage.

What children are not taught by typically falsified school textbooks is that the marriage of this Englishman to this "Indian" was not a unique occurrence. During the following decades and centuries, such marriages happened frequently, resulting in innumerable descendants, many of whom merged with the "white" population and many who merged with the indigenous population.[116] Also, the "success" of Rolfe's marriage presents the transformation of an "Indian" into "white" culture, consistent with a colonialist mentality.

Equally important, but hardly ever told, is the story of Eunice Williams, an English woman who was captured by Mohawks and chose to live with them, married a Mohawk and had children with him. She could not be persuaded to return to her English family.[117] There were other indigenous "Indians" who followed the example of Pocahontas, but there were also many "whites" who followed the example of Eunice Williams,[118] as well as many others creating mixed couples among "Indians," "whites," and "blacks" who lived in both "Indian" and non-"Indian" communities.

For example, in the New England colonies in the eighteenth

century, there were many intermixtures of indigenous "Indians," "blacks," and "whites." In Connecticut, "Indian" slaves and "black" slaves intermarried to the point where the "Indians" lost their identity. Since some of the "blacks" were themselves "mulattos," many of these mixtures were three-way mixtures. Similar mixtures occurred in Rhode Island and Massachusetts. Dukes County, Massachusetts, which includes Martha's Vineyard, was populated with mixtures of "Indians," "blacks," and "whites." Free "Indian" women also married "black" and "mulatto" men, some of whom were slaves and some of whom were free.[119] Throughout the eighteenth century, some "Indian" groups in New England added outsiders, both "white" and "black," to their communities through marriage.[120]

Similar events happened elsewhere. In Virginia, in the eighteenth and early nineteenth centuries, "people of all colors in Virginia and elsewhere mixed to some extent."[121] In some cases non-"Indians" ("whites," "blacks," and "white"-"black" mixtures) and persons of mixed "Indian" plus non-"Indian" ancestry joined the "Indian" communities. In some cases they merged into the "white" communities and in some cases they merged into "black" communities.[122]

In the seventeenth century in South Carolina, British "white" immigrants owned both "black" and "Indian" slaves and had children with both. In the following generation, many of these "white"-"black" offspring and "white"-"Indian" offspring mixed together and had "white"-"black"-"Indian" children.[123] In the eighteenth century in Georgia, escaped "black" slaves joined local "Indian" communities and became a part of them.[124]

Many indigenous tribes had "black" slaves. The Seminole freed their slaves after Emancipation, and the slaves became equal tribal members with no boundaries to marriage among them. This harmony continued for over 100 years.[125]

In the seventeenth and early eighteenth centuries, some Cherokees were known to have owned "black" slaves. As was typical of most slave owners, this ownership resulted in children with "black" mothers and the masters as biological fathers. In southern Kentucky, for example, slave children of African-Cherokee mixture joined with slave children of African-English mixture, and after the Civil War they obtained land in the hills to form a community. During its survival of nearly hundred years, this community accepted some "white" women who were rejected by their own communities or families, and some of these women merged with the community and had children. As this community slowly disintegrated during the twentieth century, its former inhabitants scattered and moved into northern cities, notably Indianapolis, Chicago, Gary, Ft. Wayne, Dayton, and Kansas City, Kansas, and some of their descendants have further scattered across the United States.[126]

Genetic studies of various isolated groups in southeastern United States reveal mixtures of European, "Indian," and African ancestry dating as far back as the late seventeenth century. Some members of these groups left their communities and married into the larger society, often marrying "whites."[127]

In the nineteenth century, Montana was a scene of many marriages between European settlers and the local "Indians."[128] But there was nothing unusual about this in that part of the country. "Intermarriage between white men and native women was found everywhere throughout the continent where Europeans and their descendants sought animal skins, from the valley of the St. Lawrence to the far Southwest, from the Great Lakes to the Rocky Mountains."[129] These marriages were so common among fur traders that it became unusual for a fur trader not to married to an "Indian."[130]

In one example, a person living in Arizona described his grandparents as indigenous Americans. His maternal grandparents were Hopi. His paternal grandfather was a light-skinned indigenous American with ancestry from two tribes who managed to live as a "white" man. He married a woman of Dutch and German ancestry. The speaker, a mixture of three indigenous American tribes along with Dutch and German, married a woman from Ireland.[131]

Just as the Hemings family illustrates the merging of "white" and "black," so does the family of Charles Brent Curtis illustrate some of the merging of Europeans and indigenous Americans. Curtis, regarded as the first person with significant "Indian" ancestry to hold next to the highest office in the land, became the thirty-first Vice President of the United States in 1929. Curtis' father was an American whose English ancestors arrived in America in the early 1600s. Curtis's maternal great-grandmother's ancestors were from three different tribes of indigenous peoples, and his maternal great-grandfather's ancestors were a mixture of indigenous people and French Canadian. Curtis's maternal grandfather was of French ancestry. Thus, Curtis's ancestors were English, French, and indigenous peoples. During his early childhood, he lived on a Kansa reservation. He married an American of European ancestry and had three children.[132]

So were Curtis and his children "white" or "Indian"? It is a senseless question—except to expose the lie of "racial" purity.

Thus, we have America where everyone is potentially of mixed ancestry from Africans, indigenous peoples, and Asians, and also ancestry from Europeans from many different countries, where these countries have various ancestral backgrounds. Indigenous Americans came from Asia, and many of them also have ancient European genes.[133] The idea that Americans can be neatly divided up into biological "races" is a combination of ignorance, myths and lies.

Chapter 5

World Intimacies from Ancient Times

One of the remarkable documents of human history is Claudius Ptolemy's set of maps of the world as seen from Eurasia almost two thousand years ago.[134] These maps and the accompanying text reveal an awareness of a diverse, multicultural world extending from the northern British Isles to China and Indonesia to south of the equator in Africa. His maps and text reveal the extent to which people had traveled, traded, and collected detailed information, including interaction with local populations in distant lands, by the second century CE (AD).

Claudius Ptolemy (ca. 90-168 CE) lived in Alexandria in the Roman province of Egypt. His comprehensive map of the world has the Persian Gulf as its center. To the northwest it extends as far as Great Britain, Ireland, and small islands to the north of Ireland. To the west it shows some small islands some distance west of Africa above the equator, probably the Cape Verde islands. America, of course, was not known to Ptolemy's world. To the east, the map extends to the east of Malaysia and Indonesia and shows great rivers going from north to south in the far east of Asia that appear to include the Mekong River. To the south, Africa is shown extending below the equator, with details showing some of the lakes feeding the White Nile River south of the equator. West Africa is also shown below the equator. The accuracy of the map declines at its extremes, but, nonetheless, its resemblance to the entire

Eastern Hemisphere as we know it today is remarkable.

What is even more remarkable are the details that the accompanying text provides of the people living in the areas of the map's outer reaches. Both the maps and the descriptions of the people, animals and foliage show that Ptolemy's sources were quite familiar, for example, with the interior of Africa above and below the equator. These sources did not remain on their sailing vessels or along the coast, but ventured far inland and stayed long enough to describe in detail what they observed. Thus the interior of sub-Saharan Africa was known in Ptolemy's time long before the European ventures and search for slaves that dominated the 16th to 19th centuries.

These maps and their accompanying texts reveal what had been occurring throughout the world in the preceding and subsequent centuries, namely that people traveled long distances and interacted with and traded with other people far from their own homes.

Is it likely that these travelers were celibates who never had sex with the local people they visited? In the previous chapter, we saw how quickly some of the English colonists had children with the local population and with the new African arrivals. No evidence has been produced to show that the English, men and women, in the seventeenth century had a greater sexual appetite than people elsewhere in the world. It is reasonable to assume that what happened then and there was not some odd exception in history, but the norm.

Thus, the world history of commerce, travel and military adventurism has a direct bearing on the extent to which different groups most likely intermingled intimately and produced "mixed" children.

Following is a small sampling of cross-group interactions throughout recorded history—a tiny fraction of the whole—prior to the development of modern concepts of "race." In many of these samples, cross-group sex and marriages were known to have occurred. In others, it is reasonable to presume that they probably occurred. The extent of these ancient interactions reveals the absurdity of defining rigid "races" based on observations of people only two hundred years ago.

Human Trade and Travel over Millennia

By fifteen thousand years ago, humans had migrated to all parts of the globe.[135] Separated by physical distance, bodies of water, mountains and climate, human groups in different places developed different cultures over thousands of years. But using animals, boats and legs, people in one group would travel and interact with other groups. That has been the way it has been for many millennia.[136] "Cross-cultural encounters have been a regular feature of world history since the earliest days of the human species' existence."[137]

New discoveries about human interactions are constantly being made, so more will be known later than is known today. We know now that for thousands of years, cross-cultural contact and trade was very prevalent in the Mediterranean area connecting southern Europe, Asia Minor, southwestern Asia and northern Africa. At least as far back as 9000 years ago, around 7000 BCE (BC), boats traveled along the Mediterranean. Evidence of boat trade between different populations along the Mediterranean goes back to 6500 BCE. Various items uniquely produced in one area would show up elsewhere hundreds of miles away. Evidence dated in the fourth and fifth millennia BCE shows seashells from the Indian Ocean in Mesopotamia, an area that includes present-day Iraq. Evidence dated in the third millennium BCE reveals bowls made in Mesopotamia appearing in Uzbekistan.[138]

That trade over land across long distances should occur by the third millennium BCE is not surprising when we take into consideration that by then the swiftly moving horse and camel had been domesticated and used for travel. Many millennia before then, donkey caravans were used for transport. [139]

Trade in Egypt up and down the Nile and across the Red Sea occurred prior to 2000 BCE. In addition, there was trade between Egyptians and Lebanese. Egyptian trade extended as far south as Punt in Africa (an area west of the southern part of the Red Sea in what is now Eritrea), northeastern Sudan and northern Ethiopia. Phoenicians occupying coastal areas centered in what is now Lebanon and Syria traded with the Nile delta region and westward to Greece prior to 1000 BCE. During the first millennium BCE, Phoenician trade extended as far west as southern Spain and Morocco. One of the Phoenician outposts was Carthage, located in what is now Tunisia, which later became an independent, powerful city-state before its destruction by the Romans in the second century BCE. In the fifth century BCE, Carthaginians, in search of trade, sailed to the Atlantic and down the west coast of Africa, establishing settlements in Morocco and possibly further south.[140]

During the first millennium BCE, there was widespread immigration to Greece, so that by the fourth century BCE, the estimated number of non-Greeks in Greece was almost equal to one-half the number of Greek citizens. Greeks also settled elsewhere, and Greek colonies extended into what is now Spain and France to the west and the Black Sea in the east, and south to Egypt and Libya in the area of Benghazi. These Greek colonies also served as trading diasporas across these regions. This dispersion of Greeks occurred before Alexander of Macedon ("the Great") began his conquests.[141]

Due to conquests by Alexander in the fourth century BCE, Greeks and Hellenic cultural influences extended far into Asia and Africa and merged with the local cultures. Alexander's conquests (at times extremely brutal including massacring entire populations and enslaving surviving women)[142] and those of his successors took them across Persia to northwest India and south to the Indian Ocean. A Greek state was established in Bactria in present-day northern Afghanistan near Tajikistan. The Greek "conquest of Bactria brought Greeks, Persians, Indians, and others into close relationships."[143] The Greeks established a diaspora trade community in the Buddhist center of Gandhara in what is now northern Pakistan and northeastern Afghanistan. In these areas cultures blended and altered art, political structures, religion and philosophy, with influences going in both directions.[144] During this time the Gandhara region "was home to a cosmopolitan population with roots in Greece, India, and East Asia."[145] Alexander's conquests also took him into northern Africa into Egypt and as far west as the Ammon oasis near Egypt's western border (now called Siwa).[146]

Alexander's conquests displaced the prior Persian rule that had existed over much of the territory that he and his successors conquered.[147] After the conquests had been completed, Alexander "encouraged his veterans to marry Persian women in order to facilitate the integration of the two societies."[148] Alexander himself took a Persian noble woman as his concubine.[149] Later he married the daughter of a nobleman who was located in an area that is now shared by Tajikistan and Uzbekistan.[150]

As we shall see, the idea that the conquerors should marry into the local population was not unique to Alexander. Thomas Jefferson, for example, suggested a similar process to bring about peace between European colonists and "Indians."[151] An American "Indian" chief had encouraged the same practice to bring about peace with the invading Europeans.[152] The marriage of Pocahontas and John Rolfe, a marriage of love, was accepted by Chief Powhatan and the English authorities as a way to establish peace between their respective groups.[153] Such arrangements in the interests of peace were common throughout human history, evidence of the universal power of sexual union and family. More examples follow in this chapter.

Cultural interactions and blendings did not require invasions or the march of soldiers. The "silk road" was the name for several alternative routes connecting eastern China to Uzbekistan, Turkmenistan, India, the Middle East, Egypt, eastern Africa, southern Europe and points in between. These routes were used primarily for peaceful trade and spiritual pursuits. More will be said about the silk road below.

Empires and the Question of "Civilization"

The expansion by invasions of the Roman empire that began in the first century BCE, and invasions into that empire from elsewhere, resulted in cultural interactions across southern Europe, northern Africa and central Asia extending over several centuries. These were not interactions between the civilized Romans and uncivilized "barbarians" as is often thought, but between and among different civilizations with differing views of what constitutes being civilized.

To say this is to question the very meaning of "civilization" and to rethink what historians have written. How one views "civilization" and the place of violence in creating new social orders are factors in how or whether one ranks different cultures. In looking at the formation of new social orders, we will see that it is not about "races" but about processes that merge people who were formerly separate.

For example, if "civilization" is thought to include coordinated social organization on a large scale, that was accomplished around 2500 years before the Roman empire with the construction of the pyramids in Egypt. The Great Pyramid of Khufu remained the tallest human-made structure in the world for nearly 4,000 years. The construction of the pyramids required organization of tens of thousands of workers and artisans, along with precise engineering, mathematical expertise, and planning.[154]

In the first millennium BCE, Carthage (in what is now Tunisia) grew into a wealthy city that was no less "civilized" than Rome. Carthage became the ruling center of the Carthaginian empire that stretched across northern Africa from Libya to the east to the Atlantic Ocean to the west, and extended into the southern half of Spain and Portugal.[155] The Phoenicians who developed and expanded Carthage's control did so initially through trade and settlement and later by military conquest.[156] The Romans completely destroyed Carthage in the third of three wars.[157] Did Rome's greater military power entitle it to be regarded as the more advanced civilization? Without the Phoenicians, this book would not look like it does now. "All western script stands on the foundation of the Phoenician alphabet."[158]

In terms of size, cultural influence, and the interactions among many different ethnicities, the huge Achaemenid Persian empire, which lasted for over two centuries in the sixth to fourth centuries BCE, must be considered to be as important as the Greek and Roman empires that followed. That Persian empire extended east to the Indus River that flows through what is now the center of Pakistan, northeast into what is now Kazakhstan, west to the Danube River in Central Europe, and across much of northern Africa, including Egypt and Libya. Numerous ethnic groups were under its wing, including ethnic Ethiopians and Nubians.[159]

Empires are often thought to indicate "civilization." During the first few centuries CE, the Iranian-speaking nomadic Alans, who had no empire, were in one respect quite civilized in that they did not own slaves.[160] In those times most societies, including the Greeks and Romans, did have slaves.[161] Why do we so often think today that slave-holding empires were among the most "civilized" ones of the past? A way of life that did not embody slavery was perhaps more civilized.

Do we consider civilization to reflect advanced technology?

By the first century CE, the Gauls, often still referred to by today's historians as "barbarians," had some farming implements that were much more technologically advanced than those of the Romans, among them a mechanical reaper, at a time when ninety percent of the economy depended on agriculture. Scandinavians built better ships. Germans were better at metalwork and made better weapons.[162] The remarkable Roman-built aqueducts were preceded by the remarkable Persian qanat network, built hundreds of years before the Roman empire emerged.[163] The production of glass and artistic objects made of glass have been traced back to Egypt and Mesopotamia four to over five thousand years ago.[164] We've already mentioned the technological skills required to build the pyramids in Egypt.

As for medicine, Egyptian doctors were recognized by Homer around the eighth century BCE as the most advanced.[165] Important developments in mathematics occurred in ancient Egypt, Mesopotamia, India and China as well as in ancient Greece.[166] The introduction of the sine function, essential for trigonometry, came from India.[167]

One of the most underrated technological achievements underlying the advance of civilization was the invention and production of paper. Paper made it much easier to preserve and spread the ideas that shaped the world, ideas so important that they survived the frequent burning of the paper on which they were written. Paper was invented in China in the second century BCE.[168]

During these early times, the "barbarian" German tribes showed many signs of civilized life. They made plows and spades, pottery, and musical instruments; they styled their hair and sometimes dyed it. Men shaved. Much clothing was woven and fabrics were dyed. Their smelting of iron was equal to the work of the Roman smiths. Their artwork was well developed. Jewelry and other ornaments, including gold and silver ones, were intricately designed. They were initially not good at brutalities of warfare, even though they made technically superior weapons. "Barbarian" Scandinavian craftsmen made masterful metalwork art. The "barbarian" Huns brought to Europe artistic metalwork designs and techniques from Asia.[169]

As for governmental stability, nearly half of Rome's fifty emperors during the first, second and third centuries CE were assassinated. Rome had four emperors in just one year, 69 CE, two of whom were murdered that year; it had three emperors in 193 CE, two of whom were murdered that year; it had six emperors in 238 CE, four of whom were killed that year and the sixth assassinated later. In the twenty-year period from 455 CE to 475 CE, the Western empire had ten emperors, most of them killed by rivals.[170] In contrast, King Genseric (Geiseric) governed the "barbarian" Vandals and Alans in the fifth century CE for nearly fifty years, longer than any Roman emperor, and died of natural causes at the age of 88.[171]

As for cruelty, the norms of ancient times, whether Roman or non-Roman, are shocking to us today. Human sacrifices and massacres of civilians were common.[172] The Roman empire became what it was in part by massacres of entire populations.[173] Is that what we mean by "civilization?" "It is important to pause and reflect for a moment on the sheer terror and ruthless destruction that marked the acquisition of the Roman empire."[174]

In short, in terms of "civilization," the hierarchical distinction usually made between the Roman empire and "barbarians" is false. In fairness to the "barbarians," some of this history is gradually being rewritten, though the biased term "barbarian" remains in use.[175]

The Roman empire was but one of many empires that at various times occupied and connected Europe, Asia and Africa. It is only a common bias that has treated the Roman empire as more significant than the others. Still, due to the current state of our historical knowledge (which is still being altered and grown by archeological evidence), the rise and fall of the Roman empire and the resulting and subsequent interactions among different peoples is a good focal point to aid our understanding of the mixture of cultures and peoples in what is now Europe, North Africa, East Africa, the Middle East, and southern, central and east Asia. Of equal importance, treated below, are the interactions that occurred across Asia and extended into Europe and

Africa.

The Roman Empire and its Demise

As for the Roman empire and its interactions, here are but a few of the innumerable highlights.

The expansion of Rome beyond Italy began in the third century BCE, about two hundred years before Julius Caesar conquered Gaul (France and Belgium).[176] At its height in the second century CE, the Roman empire completely surrounded the Mediterranean Sea, extending northwest to Hadrian's Wall in the north of England, west to include what is now Spain, Portugal and Morocco, east to the southeastern corner of the Black Sea (though not anywhere near as far east as the land Alexander had controlled) and south down the Nile to the border of Egypt and Sudan. The empire included all of northern Africa along the Mediterranean, southern and western Europe up to the Rhine and Danube rivers (including all of what is now Portugal, Spain and France, western and southern parts of Germany, most of Austria, all of Greece, the western half of Hungary, all of Serbia, much of Romania above the Danube and all of Bulgaria), and extending to the east and south to include nearly all of Turkey, much of Syria, all of Lebanon and Israel, most of Egypt and a small portion of northern Sudan. There were also many Roman incursions beyond these boundaries.[177]

The largest beginning of this expansion was the destruction of Carthage and its influence. It took them three wars (the "Punic wars") to destroy Carthage. The first of these began in 264 BCE, initiated by Rome to reclaim Sicily.[178] That war, which broke long-standing treaties between Rome and Carthage,[179] spawned the development of one of Rome's biggest obstacles.

That obstacle was Hannibal who, beginning around 218 BCE, set out to destroy Rome on behalf of Carthage. Hannibal's father, Hamilcar Barca, had begun the campaign to gain Carthaginian control of the southern half of Spain and Portugal after the first Punic war. Hamilcar's family came from an area of Africa that is now in Libya. Father and son had in common a hatred of Rome. After his father's death, Hannibal, accompanied by his brother-in-law until the latter's death, trekked, with tens of thousands of soldiers, from Spain through southern Gaul (France) into Italy, crossing the Alps with the aid of elephants. Hannibal reached Rome, destroying a huge Roman army on the way with clever military tactics, but did not enter the city. His soldiers advanced through Italy down to its toe and remained for about fifteen years before Hannibal, weary and lacking the support of Carthage, began a retreat. Hannibal's soldiers consisted of Africans, Spaniards, Phoenicians, Gauls, Italians, and Greeks.[180]

It is not likely that these soldiers remained celibate during their extended visit. As was true then, before and afterward, "Men at war avail themselves of whatever sexual opportunities that arise."[181] The elite apparently did likewise. Hasdrubal, a member of Hamilcar's family who took over the Carthaginian mission in Spain following Hamilcar's death, married the daughter of a Spanish king. Later, Hannibal too married a member of the Spanish elite.[182]

The retreat of Hannibal and the destruction of Carthage was followed by Rome's expansion into the areas formerly under Carthage's control. Around the same time Rome began its expansion eastward. By the middle of the second century CE, the empire had extended to the east and south as noted above.[183]

The expansion of Rome was aided by African soldiers formerly under Carthage's command. Rome expanded into England with the aid of Africans. It has been estimated that between ten and twenty-five percent of the 300,000 Roman troops occupying Britain after the Roman invasion of 43 CE were Africans. Intermarriage between the male occupiers and British women was legally permitted by 197 CE, but this just made legal what had already been occurring. Many of the occupying troops did not return home but remained in England.[184] Thus, Hannibal and his many thousands of soldiers were not the only sources of the insertion of African genetic material into Europe during those times.

Across the vast area under Rome's control, roads were built to connect its various parts. Commerce by ship throughout the Mediterranean linked Italy and Sicily to western Spain beyond the

Strait of Gibraltar, to the rebuilt Carthage in Tunisia, to Alexandria in Egypt, to Greece, to Gaza, Israel and Syria, and to Turkey. Alexandria also was linked by ship to Syria, Turkey, Cyrene (Libya) and France in addition to all of the eastern coast of the Adriatic Sea. In addition, trade by ship went beyond the empire through the Black Sea to its northern shore. Through these routes, Africa fed the empire with grain; Spain, Africa and Syria supplied much of the olive oil, and wine was supplied from several places. Shipping and roads connected the various parts of the empire with one another, from east to west, north to south. Thus, traders and sailors from various parts of the empire interacted.[185]

These connections were not enough for the wealthy, who had more exotic tastes for Chinese silks, Southeast Asian spices, and Arabian incense. These goods were obtained using sea routes that connected the empire to India and Southeast Asia, and overland "silk road" routes that connected the empire to eastern China.[186] To facilitate this trade, Roman diasporas were established in southern India.[187] The trade networks between India and the Roman empire interacted with the Ethiopian highland kingdom of Aksum, a kingdom that included parts of Yemen across the strait. The Aksum kingdom converted to Christianity in the fourth century and was an early source of Christianity in Ethiopia. Architecture and wall inscriptions in this region show the influences of India, Syria and Greece.[188]

The lines currently dividing the three continents of Europe, Asia and Africa are relatively recent phenomena created by agreement. Viewed from today's perspective, the Roman empire included northern Africa and parts of western Asia, so that any conceptual separation of these three continents were probably of little relevance to the Roman empire or the preceding empires. The African-centered Carthaginian empire included much of Spain, and only the easily navigated nine-mile wide Strait of Gibraltar separates this part of Europe from Africa. Even the sea of 100 or so miles separating Africa from Sicily was regularly navigated for trade and war.

Similarly, the Persian empire included parts of what we now consider to be Africa, so it is unlikely that any continental division between Africa and Asia would have been relevant to that empire. Thus, what seems separate to us today was not necessarily separate in the past.

The Roman empire, like the empires that preceded it, embraced many ethnicities.[189] Roman emperors and other officials and leaders did not all come from Rome or Italy. In 193 CE, Septimus Severus became emperor of the Roman empire. He was born in Africa (Libya). His second wife was from Syria. Their two sons followed him as emperors. In 217, Macrinus became emperor. He was a Moor born in a city that is now Cherchell, Algeria. In 218, Elagabalus became emperor. He was born in Syria. He had three wives (sequentially) and many lovers, male and female. In 222, Alexander Severus became emperor. He was born in Lebanon. In 244, Philip the Arab, born in Syria, became emperor. In 253, Aemilius Aemilianus became emperor. He was born on the African island of Jerba.[190]

The mixing of different people and ethnicities within the empire later became a mixing of people within the empire with those outside the empire, especially as the empire sought accommodation with outside forces in its failed efforts to preserve itself.[191] Among these accommodations, Sarus was one of several Gothic nobles who served as Roman generals.[192] The top Roman general Stilicho had Vandal ancestry.[193] Since some of these men rose to the top from below, it is fair to assume that many others like them remained at lower ranks (and probably lived longer). When the Gothic king Radagaisus invaded Italy in 405-406 and was defeated, many of his remaining troops were brought into the Roman army.[194] The Franks also added to the Roman military, and several became commanders.[195]

After years of internal instability and turmoil, the empire collapsed when accommodations reached their limits and groups from the north, mostly Germanic, invaded.[196] These invasions were mainly precipitated by the incursions into Europe by the Huns from Asia, as the German groups sought to escape from them.[197] The first main incursion into the empire began in 375-376, when a Germanic group (Goths) crossed the Danube in what is now Bulgaria.[198] Within a few years Germanic groups had invaded Greece, the Balkans and Italy, and later moved westward all the way to Spain.[199] One of the most ominous incidents for the empire occurred in 410, when Goths entered Rome and engaged in rape and pillage.[200]

As the Goths moved from east to west, another Germanic group, the Vandals, along with Iranian-speaking Alans and other Germanic groups came down from the north and east into France and Spain. The Vandals and Alans, in spite of their language differences, joined together and, under pressure from the Visigoths who were also moving into France and Spain, headed into northern Africa from west to east all the way to Carthage and the surrounding area, where they settled. The movement of these groups included families, not just soldiers.[201]

The Huns came from Asia, but it is not clear from exactly where. They were nomads who occupied areas in the Eurasian Steppe. The problem of determining where they came from is that the Eurasian Steppe is a dry region including grasslands that extends thousands of miles from eastern Europe into Mongolia and far into China. Their origins within that vast region are uncertain. Their reasons for moving westward are also unclear.[202] What is known is that they looked quite unfamiliar to those who recorded what they saw.[203]

Initially, in the last quarter of the fourth century, the Huns moved westward towards the Roman empire not as organized conquerors but as independent bands of skilled horse-riding archers without a common leader.[204] In some initial battles with Goths, some Huns were recruited by a Goth leader to fight other Huns.[205] It was not until several decades later, in 441, that Attila became the Huns' commander and chief.[206] For over a decade, Attila's Huns dominated much of Europe from Istanbul (then, Constantinople) to the outskirts of Paris, creating a short-lived Hunnic empire. Moving out from their new heartland in the area of Hungary, they dominated the Balkans and invaded Greece almost as far south as Athens. They then moved west into northern Italy and captured Milan. Another contingent moved west into Gaul (France) after crossing the Rhine at Coblenz (Koblenz), Germany. In Gaul the Huns were repulsed, and they retreated.[207]

Although the Huns were as brutal in warfare as their predecessors, they made accommodations and agreements with the people they had invaded or threatened to invade. They adopted some of the characteristics of those they had conquered, including dressing like those they had subjugated. They adopted Germanic languages.[208] They accepted subsidies from the Romans as part of agreements and treaties, gathering lots of gold in the process. They formed alliances with Alans and various Germanic groups in their campaigns against Romans and other Germanic groups. Using a combination of violent intimidation, purchasing of services with the gold they received in payments to ward off their aggressions, and even marriages, they expanded by incorporating others.[209]

Attila died in 453 by drinking too much at a marriage party where he had taken yet another wife.[210] The Hunnic empire collapsed within a few years after that, and remaining Hunnic groups disintegrated. What happened to the Huns after that? Given the Huns' manner of adopting some of the characteristics of the people they had conquered, it is likely that the reason they disappeared is that over time they merged into the surrounding populations. There is no evidence that they migrated back to Asia.[211]

By 476 the western Roman empire had collapsed.[212] Attila and the Huns were directly and indirectly a primary precipitating force in causing that collapse.[213] The turmoil of Europe during those times and subsequently led many separate groups to form alliances that over time resulted in larger groups and varying degrees of absorption of the smaller groups into the larger ones.[214]

What we see here from ancient and pre-ancient times, including the period of the Roman empire, is that people from Europe, Asia and Africa interacted through trade, warfare and empires. There were no lasting barriers that prevented sex across group lines, and group identities themselves changed as new groups were created. Cross-group marriage and sex were sometimes advocated as a way to facilitate peaceful integration of different groups. There was nothing new or unique about that. The wife of a Hunnic ruler offered attractive Hun women to some Roman ambassadors for the night, and though the offer reportedly was declined, it probably indicated a common practice.[215] Brutal cross-group sex was also a typical byproduct of war, as soldiers everywhere are known to rape when they conquer.[216]

Cross-group marriages at high levels were not uncommon. Romans and "barbarians" intermarried. A daughter of the Roman emperor Valentinian III, Eudocia, married the son of the king of the Vandals as part of a peace deal.[217] A high Roman military commander, Ricimer, had a grandfather who was a Visigothic king, and his mother was descended from a princess of another Germanic group, the Suevi.[218] He married the daughter of Anthemius, who was a Roman general and emperor from 467-472.[219] A Visigothic ruler, Athaulf, married Galla Placidia, the western emperor Honorius' sister, as part of his strategy to get an advantageous settlement with the Romans.[220] A daughter of Galla Placidia, Iulia Grata Honoria, offered herself to Attila for marriage. (He declined, since he already had several wives, and his ventures took him elsewhere.)[221] That the offer was made, even though it was exceptional, indicates that the idea of cross-group marriages was present.

Since recorded cross-group marriages and sex occurred at the highest levels, it is fair to assume that it occurred at lower levels as well, beneath the attention of those whose writings survived. As noted above, many non-Roman people entered the Roman empire and Roman armies at various levels, so the opportunities for cross-group marriages were certainly present. This history clearly indicates that the Europeans of today are a mixture of many different groups going not only back to the Roman empire but also before, and that those groups included Africans and Asians. The Roman empire was neither the beginning nor the end of such mixtures.

A look at the development and fall of the Roman empire gives us a general picture of how different peoples and groups merged to form new groups and new cultures. But we would be quite mistaken if we regarded these events in Europe as constituting the center of the world during those times. Much was going on in the Americas prior to 1492 about which we know relatively little; we do know that the Americas had been occupied by migrants from Asia for thousands of years.[222] We know more about what was happening in the Eastern Hemisphere. What we see are variations on the same theme, that through migrations, explorations, trade, war, marriages, and spiritual quests, people from different cultures interacted and different cultures merged and combined to form new cultures and new combinations.[223] It is the same today; during our short lives we can see it in slow motion.

The "Silk Road"

A primary facilitator of these early combinations in Europe, Asia and Africa, beginning over two thousand years ago, was the so-called "silk road." It was a not a "road" but a multiple of various alternative routes, including routes by sea, that linked eastern and central Europe to central, eastern and southeastern Asia, Asia Minor and eastern Africa. As such, the silk road was more of an expression of interconnection than a particular route. For many centuries the silk road formed important linkages among the three continents. The silk road connected eastern China, Mongolia, Turkestan, northern India, Persia, Asia Minor, Egypt and intermediate places to southern and eastern Europe. The land routes went as far east as Chang'an (Xi'an) (about 600 miles southwest of Beijing) and later to the East China Sea at Hangzhou (near Shanghai).

By the first century BCE, regular travel by sea connected ports in southeastern Asia, Japan, and Korea, to India, Persia, Arabia, Egypt, and eastern Africa. The silk road's development has been traced back to the third and second centuries BCE, but there is evidence that the links began to develop long before then.[224]

It is unlikely that anyone traveled the full distance, a distance of over four thousand miles if flown by a super-fit crow, in those early days. Instead, there were linkages among settled and nomadic peoples that enabled trade to occur relay-style between the road's extremities.[225] But in addition to trade, people traveled for other reasons. "Refugees, artists, craftsmen, missionaries, robbers, and envoys all made their way along these routes."[226] In many cases travel could not be explained in purely economic terms, as people also pursued cultural and spiritual ends: religion, technology and art spread throughout the vast area.[227]

Archeological discoveries are still being made, so more will be known later than is known now. The most recent discoveries indicate an age-old intermingling of different cultures and peoples across Eurasia.[228] For example, well-preserved bodies in a desert site in northwest China revealed the presence of a mixed population of fair-haired, pale skinned males over six feet tall along with shorter Chinese.

These bodies were three to four thousand years old. The tall men wore clothing similar to that worn then in Ireland. How this happened is currently just a matter of speculation.[229]

Also in the second millennium BCE, more than 3000 years ago, trade apparently occurred that connected coastal people, directly or indirectly, to an area of northern China more than 2000 miles by land travel from any coast. There was also trade over 2500 years ago linking people living in China and people in Siberia a thousand miles or more to the north.[230]

The Xinjiang region in northwestern China seems to have been a place where many different peoples mingled. Immigrants from Gandhara (an area in present-day Pakistan and Afghanistan) introduced their written language to the people of this region of China in the second and third centuries CE. The immigrants stayed and married into the local population.[231] Inscriptions left along the mountain roads between these two areas were made in the Iranian, Chinese, Tibetan and Hebrew languages.[232]

In the fourth century CE a Buddhist translator, Kumarajiva, traveled as others did between Gandhara and Kucha in the Xinjiang region. He was the son of an Indian prince; his mother was a sister of a Kucha king.[233] Although the translator had taken vows of celibacy, they were as effective then as now, and it was reported that he had fathered several children with local women in China.[234] From the third to seventh centuries CE, Turfan in this same region was a place where Chinese, Iranians and Uighurs lived together.[235]

Conflicts between groups inevitably occurred. In some known cases, cross-group marriages were sought as one of the means of bringing conflicting groups into peaceful relations. For example, in the third and second centuries BCE, the Chinese Han empire came into conflict with the Turkish-speaking nomads occupying the Mongolian steppes, the Xiongnu (Hsiung-nu). In an attempt to create more peaceful relations, dynastic marriages were arranged between Han princesses and Xiongnu leaders. Of course, such tactics did not always work as planned, but they were tried.[236]

During the violent conflicts that followed, some of the Xiongnu merged with the Chinese; some of the Chinese merged with the

Xiongnu; the Chinese adopted some of the dress, music and dance of the Xiongnu; and the Xiongnu adopted some of the agricultural techniques of the Chinese. During some of these attempts to expand trade westward, a noted Han ambassador, Zhang Qian, married a Xiongnu woman and had a son.[237]

Marriages, of course, were not merely political tools but involved the fulfillment of sexual attractions. We may never know the extent to which sex and sexual desire have altered history. Historians have usually attempted to explain significant events in non-sexual, materialistic, political, or spiritual terms, ignoring the role of the most prevalent of human passions. The influence of Plato, Aristotle and subsequent theology is evident among these historians, including Marxist ones, as they seek to explain important events without reference to the "lower" emotions.[238] Yet, these "lower emotions," whether the passions of love or hate, of cooperating or conquering, are, for better or worse, what makes us human.

As indicated in the previous chapter, sexual emotions were ingrained in the United States' "southern way of life." I suspect the unexpressed power of sexual emotions was not unique to this instance. Given how often conquering soldiers everywhere rape the conquered, we might ponder how often soldiers are more driven by the desire to kill the men so they can have the women than by some idealistic goal of destroying evil empires or expanding good ones.

The role of sex in history has surely been underestimated.

The Middle Ages

According to the legends recorded by Washington Irving,[239] sex altered the history of Spain and Portugal. Whether sex was the cause or not, the history of this area was certainly altered by the invasion of Moors from Africa in the eighth century.

According to these legends, a beautiful Moorish princess landed on the shores of Spain when the ship she was on went astray in a storm. She ended up in the king's palace. The Christian king sought her intimate company, but she repeatedly turned him away. The exasperated king then forced himself upon her. She was able to send a letter describing what had happened. When the letter reached the Moors' leaders, the outraged leaders decided to invade to rescue her. The rest, as they say, is history.

The Moors were devoted to Islam. They were a mixture of Arabs from southwestern Asia and Africans. They dominated the regions that are now Spain and Portugal for several centuries, beginning in 711 CE, until Christians violently took over in the twelfth century in Portugal and during the following centuries in Spain.[240] Most of the Moors were forced out, but some managed to remain by converting to Christianity.[241] The Moors' period of domination, unlike the subsequent Christian ones in those times, was characterized by significant tolerance of other religions—Jews and Christians.[242] The beautiful Alhambra in Granada and the mosque-cathedral in Cordoba are two of the many remaining visible products of the Moors' rule.[243]

The genetic mixtures that occurred in Portugal and Spain—with ingredients from Carthaginians, Romans, Germans, Moors and others[244]—were spread around the world in the fifteenth and sixteenth centuries when Portuguese adventurers and traders seeking spices and gold (among other things) circled the globe and established trading posts, some with Portuguese diasporas. Spanish traders quickly followed.[245] Portuguese traders landed in North America, South America, western Africa, eastern Africa, India, southeast Asia, China and the Philippines.[246] In eastern Africa, they landed in Mozambique and then moved up the coast as far north as the kingdom of Abyssinia in what is now northern Ethiopia and Eritrea. Several hundred of them settled there and married local women.[247] In Brazil, the Portuguese mixed with the indigenous people, and their grown offspring established colonies in the Brazilian interior.[248]

The Moorish impact on Spain and Portugal was preceded by the movement of Arabs westward and southward. In the seventh century (several decades prior to the invasion of Spain), Arabs moved into the areas of northern Africa formerly occupied by Romans. They continued westward to Morocco, making accommodations with or defeating the local populations as they went.[249]

Arab armies also moved south into an area of Africa that is now the interior of Sudan.[250] Over the following centuries, they facilitated trade that connected eastern Africa to Asia.

For several centuries along more than 1,500 miles of the east coast of Africa, commerce and social interaction occurred between the local black-skinned occupants and Arab and Persian merchants arriving by sea. This "Land of Zanj" was where Sinbad the Sailor had his adventures in the Zanj sea as told in the ninth-century Persian stories, "One Thousand and One Nights." This coastal area stretched along what is now the coasts of Somalia, Kenya, Tanzania and Mozambique. This coast formed an important part of the commerce of the Indian Ocean and linked to the African interior as well as to eastern parts of Asia by sea and land. Through this trade the banana reached Africa from southeast Asia and wealthy African merchants received fine goods including those made from porcelain, glass and brass from as far away as India, China and Indonesia. By the early fifteenth century, Chinese merchant fleets were also arriving along this coast engaging in trade that resulted in an African giraffe being given to the emperor in Beijing. During these centuries, some Arabs settled along this coast and married local occupants.[251]

This period also involved massive movement of slaves. From the seventh through the fifteenth centuries, several million African slaves with black skins were brought northward across the Sahara into northern Africa and western Asia. Slaves were obtained and taken from this African coast to Arabia and the Persian Gulf to serve in the military, as laborers and concubines.[252] "The majority were female slaves who were bought by prosperous urban households for use as servants or concubines."[253]

As the people of Africa, Asia and southwestern Europe interacted during these times through war, travel, peaceful trade and slavery, movements of various peoples within Europe and into Europe from Asia created new mixtures of cultures and people. During the ninth and tenth centuries, Slavs spread "throughout eastern Europe"; Bulgars controlled an area that is now Bulgaria; Magyars "ravaged Europe" before retreating to Hungary; and Vikings from Sweden raided and traded as far south as Italy and as far east as the Caspian Sea.[254] A Viking colony grew to become Kiev.[255] One of the Viking's trading routes reached Bagdad.[256] "By about 920, Vikings had settled throughout northwestern Europe, most notably in northern England, eastern Ireland, and Normandy."[257] Lesser known but important groups were also involved during this transformation of Europe. Many of these groups, collaborated with and combined with others.[258] The origin of some of them was Central Asia.[259]

The ongoing influence of Asia on Europe spiked with the Mongolian invasions that began around the beginning of the thirteenth century, led by Genghis Khan. The invasions resulted in the largest empire that the world had yet seen. The Mongol empire at its peak stretched from Japan and Korea in the east to Vietnam, Burma and Indonesia in southeastern Asia to Finland and Austria in Europe. It included China, Croatia, Georgia, Hungary, Poland, and Russia. Its influence reached south to Mali in Africa. Bagdad, Budapest, Kiev and Peking (Beijing) were among the many cities taken over by the Mongols. The empire included over forty percent of the world's population. "Genghis Khan was the greatest conqueror the world has ever known."[260]

Like the "great" conquerors before him—Attila, Caesar and Alexander—Genghis led the cruel slaughter of millions of people,[261] lending further support to the view that greatness as a conqueror is contrary to greatness as a human being. Evidence indicates, however, that the empire that followed the massacres was well-administered and in some ways progressive.[262]

The Mongols tolerated different religions.[263] Women had more power and privileges than elsewhere in the world.[264] Some of them were warriors.[265] Genghis also instituted a code of laws.[266] The empire made continuous land travel from Europe to China possible.[267] Many, including Marco Polo, made the entire trip.[268] Peaceful trade occurred within the various parts of the empire and artistic influences circulated widely.[269]

The Mongols spread their genes wherever they went. As invaders, they engaged in mass rapes of conquered populations.[270] To create peace, they arranged marriages between high-ranking Mongols and high-ranking non-Mongols.[271] In general, they encouraged cross-group marriages.[272] One study found that eight percent of Turkish genes today are Mongolian.[273] The percentage greatly increases as one moves eastward from Turkey.[274]

The empire began to crumble after the death of Genghis' son, Ogodei, in 1241.[275]

I will end this chapter here, without going further to discuss the various European powers that, beginning in the seventeenth century, moved and traded around the world by sea and land and over time divided much of it into colonies. As we have seen from this chapter's very brief and incomplete overview, European colonialism occurred after the various peoples of the world had over millennia interacted through war, travel, trade, sex and marriage. If there ever had been "races" in the past (for which there is no evidence), they would have been thoroughly mixed long before anyone conceived of the modern idea of "races." These subsequent adventures and colonializations by European powers created new mixtures around the world, including the people we now call "African Americans."

Chapter 6

Intimacies Exposed by DNA

As Hitler was advancing militarily to dominate the earth with his superior "race," the scientific community had already been confronted with the realization that human genes do not combine into "races" but operate independently of one another. In other words, biological "races" do not exist. Once this became known, as it was by the late 1930s, every statement that "races" have a biological basis became not just a wrong and unproven conjecture but an assertion of myth and lies.

Hitler continued his advance. The myth killed millions of people. For political reasons, not scientific ones, the notion of biological "races" continues to survive, supported by a curious, perverted passion that does not seem to die.

That perverted passion had spread the idea of "races" based on beliefs that had never been scientifically verified. The burden of scientifically proving that "races" existed was never met. The concept of "race" was a conjecture that never had the evidence necessary to back it up.[276] No one had credibly answered Charles Darwin's questioning of the idea of distinct "races," published in 1871.[277]

In place of evidence was political and economic power. This power publicized the "race" conjecture as scientific fact. Enough publishers were part of this power elite to popularize the idea. Many writers were paid to write what the elite wanted. Many teachers questioning the idea were marginalized or fired. But the truth-seekers could not be silenced.[278]

The idea of "race" was never proven. But political and economic powers supported it. It became true due to this support. Because of this support, the burden of scientifically proving that the idea of "race" was true became unnecessary. Instead, that burden had to be borne by those who sought to prove it was false. Those who questioned the idea of "race" had to disprove what had never been soundly established.

By the late 1930s, scientists who understood genetics had met that burden of disproving the concept of "race."

The understanding of genes began with Mendel's discoveries in the 1860's. The term "gene" came into use in 1909.[279] The study of genes resulted in the realization that there are not biological "races" of humankind. As Ashley Montagu explained in his paper delivered in 1941, "It is not possible to classify the various groups of mankind" using "assemblages of characters," because genes operate independently of one another.[280] There are, thus, no biological assemblage linking genes that create "racial" clusters.[281] In 1937, this point had been demonstrated in the seminal work of Theodosius Dobzhansky, *Genetics and the Origin of Species.*[282]

Beginning in 1941, Montagu spread the word. With the support of earlier research, he confronted anthropologists with the unrefuted truth that there is no "race" gene and no naturally existing cluster of genes that could create an unchanging "race." Similarities of human physical characteristics within groups were transitory, not permanent.[283]

In 1942, Montagu published the first edition of *Man's Most Dangerous Myth: The Fallacy of Race.* This work is now in its sixth edition, published in 1997.[284] This book announced to the world what the scientists knew. Unfortunately, the world's ears were stuffed with decades of myths and lies.

Montagu's findings about "race" can be summed up simply: "The so-called 'races' are populations that merely represent different kinds of temporary mixtures of genetic materials common to all mankind."[285] Today, our advanced knowledge of DNA reaffirms what was known before 1940 about "race" and genes.[286] "Modern genetic analysis refutes any biological basis to racism."[287]

Remember from Chapter 1 that in the mid-1950's, long after it was known that "races" did not exist, a chapter of my 10th grade biology book defined the "races" of humankind without any acknowledgment that the idea had not only been questioned but refuted. This chapter purporting to be science was not science but resulted from an assertion of power by the political forces that determined what textbooks would be used in schools. That assertion of power included the power of publishers and the complicity of writers who turned fiction into nonfiction, myth into fact. Science was irrelevant, even in a science text. Hitler had been defeated, but his way of thinking was affirmed in books like those, read by school children across the nation.

When we focus on the past evils of Nazi Germany, we fail to see that the Nazis' genocidal goal was the logical consequence of racist ideology that had been developed over nearly two hundred years prior to World War II and continues to survive today.[288] The same ideology that led to Nazism led the United States government, with the backing of the U.S. Supreme Court, to incarcerate Japanese Americans beginning in 1942, based solely on their ancestry.[289] Thus, the U.S. government supported the racist ideology of the enemy it was fighting.

Indigenous Americans today still are fighting to have their representation in local governments proportional to their population.[290] The racist ideology of Nazism preceded the Nazis and still surrounds us.

Any pretension that distinct human "races" exist has been further destroyed by the recent realization that the modern human species, *Homo sapiens*, is not even a clearly distinct species that is separate from preceding human-like species. How can "races" within a species be distinct if the species itself is not distinct? Predecessors of *Homo sapiens*, the Neanderthals, not only coexisted with *Homo sapiens* for thousands of years but the two human-types had sex with one another and produced fertile mixed children.[291]

Although "new information is arriving at such a fast pace that it's difficult for even scholars to keep up,"[292] the presence of Neanderthal genes in modern humans now seems certain. Up to 4% Neanderthal DNA has been found in today's Europeans and Asians.[293]

Neanderthals appeared in Europe about 300,000 to 400,000 years ago, apparently evolved from an earlier migration of human-like beings out of Africa.[294] *Homo sapiens* migrated out of Africa later, mixed with Neanderthals probably beginning in the Middle East, and their mixtures moved east into Asia and west into Europe. For reasons not yet known, the Neanderthals disappeared about 30,000 years ago, but their genes survive in modern humans.[295]

This means that Neanderthals and *Homo sapiens* were not two separate species but related beings. The usually accepted definition of a species is "a group that can produce fertile offspring with each other and cannot do so with members of other groups."[296] Since Neanderthals and modern humans produced healthy, fertile children, by this definition they cannot be two different species. The whole concept of "species" may now be in question. "There is no definition of a species perfectly describing this case."[297] "'Species' is a concept invented by humans," and it "is not clear-cut."[298]

So the idea that humans could be divided into separate "races" is completely undermined by the fact that modern humans have not even been correctly divided into separate "species" as usually defined. Exactly how humans are to be categorized in relation to their predecessors is yet to be determined.[299]

The sexual unions of Neanderthals and Homo sapiens illustrate the power of human sexuality. Cross-group sex is part of the norm. Historically, nothing has ever completely prevented it. Cross-group children result, containing new genetic mixtures that feed the biological development of humankind.[300]

As a result of these mixtures, we are more interrelated with other humans than we probably ever realized, aside from our common African origin.

DNA analyses have proven our interrelationships often in surprising ways. We saw in Chapter 4, partially proven by DNA analysis, that Thomas Jefferson had four surviving children with Sally Hemings. Two of these children became "white" and two became "black," yet all four had the same biological parents. We know that these differences in appearances is genetically possible, just as I knew this as a child from seeing sets of twins where one twin was light-skinned and the other dark-skinned. W.E.B. Du Bois recorded that in his own family there were relatives "who do not know of their Negro blood."[301] He stated, based on his thorough inquiry into his ancestry, "Africa and Europe have been united in my family. There is nothing unusual about this. . . ."[302]

There are also the following stories of previously unknown intimacies revealed by DNA testing:

A blond, blue-eyed woman discovered she had an indigenous American ancestor (which, it turns out, did not surprise her based on photographs of her grandmother).[303] But her DNA showed that she also had African ancestors whom she did not know about.[304]

An "African-American" professor discovered that he had a Jewish grandfather and another European ancestor.[305]

A brown-haired, slightly olive skinned American woman who assumed she was "white," who had a blond, blue-eyed sister, and who had assumed that all of her ancestors were from Britain, discovered through her Y chromosomes that she—and therefore, presumably, her sister—had at least one male African ancestor from three or four generations ago. She also had some indigenous American ancestry which she had not known about.[306]

A "white" man with ancestry from South Carolina learned that there was indigenous American ancestry on his mother's side dating from about three hundred years ago.[307]

Genetic testing indicates that many of those claiming to be indigenous Americans are of mixed African, European and indigenous American ancestry not unlike most "African-Americans."[308]

A southern "white" man learned of "African-American" ancestry on his mother's side. (He refused to accept the results.)[309] Another southern "white" man whose English ancestors arrived two centuries ago, was amused but not upset when his DNA showed an African ancestor.[310]

A "white" British geneticist, Byron Sykes, found traces in his own DNA of African origin.[311] He was not surprised, because he knew that "black Africans have been coming to Britain since at least the time of the Roman Empire."[312] The African DNA could have instead come from "African-Americans" who fought on the British side in the Revolutionary War and went to Britain when the war ended. The geneticist also found in himself traces of DNA from Asia.[313]

Genetic tests of a small number of "African-American" volunteers found that all of them had some European and indigenous American ancestry.[314]

Genetic tests of a small number of "white" volunteers from the South found that all of them had some African ancestry.[315]

My son had a genetic test that revealed that he had European ancestry not only from his mother's side, which was obvious and known, but also on the male side, which includes me, my father, his father, and so on. I, of course, was not surprised by the confirmation of male European ancestry. (I know of no genetic tests on my mother's side.) I had concluded as a child that all of the "blacks" I saw, including my own family, were mixed with "white." I had also concluded (correctly) that at least some "whites" were mixed with "black."

These examples are just a small fraction of what people have learned from genetic tests.

What can we learn from what they have learned?

The terms "black" and "white" are used to emphasize a narrow range of differences between people and to perpetuate a denial of their basic sameness. While there are some Africans with truly black skin, it is rare to see black skin among the Americans we call "black." The literally correct term for "blacks" would be "browns." But since "brown" refers to a range of shades from tan to near-black, and since in the summer many "whites" become tan and even brown, being brown would not create much of a separation. Browns are called "black" or "white" to falsely exaggerate the differences.

The same is true of the term "African American." Nearly all "African Americans" have considerable European ancestry, in many cases as much as half or more. From genetic testing we also know that many "whites" have some African ancestry. Thus nearly all "African Americans" are actually African European Americans, just like many "whites." Add to this that there is considerable ancestry from indigenous Americans among "blacks" and "whites," and the fact that indigenous Americans came here from Asia, we arrive at the reality that all of us are mixtures from at least two to four continents. Given that all humans originated from Africa, there are only political and societal conventions for using terms that falsely state totally separate strains of ancestry. But the fact is that we are all multi-continental. We are all part of the same human continuum.

Still, people will see that those in segregated "black" communities look quite different from those in mostly "white" communities. Many simply assume that this is visible evidence of "races." They assume this only because they have been falsely taught that "races" exist. In other words, you have to believe that "races" exist in order to think that you see them.

But what you see is a temporary and transitory piece of hundreds of thousand years of human development and interaction.

It is as if you looked out the window and saw that it was a cloudy rainy day and concluded that it had always been cloudy and rainy. It often feels that way.

It is a simple error to attribute what you see now to "forever." The race theorists committed this most simple of childish errors. Just as the weather is dynamic, ever-changing, and not static, "'Race' is a dynamic, not a static condition."[316]

This error also occurs if we think that the different physical appearances of people in different regions of the world are proof of the existence of "races." Due to genetic mutations and varying adaptations to different environments, any group whose members have mated mostly among themselves over hundreds and thousands of years will develop physical traits that differ from those of other groups. For example, the geographical origin of east Asians can usually be identified by their appearance. East Asians generally differ in appearance from south Asians, and so on. The problem with assigning "race" to these physical differences is that they are points on a continuum containing infinite variations. In addition, the assigned "race" will disappear if the group merges with another group to create different points on the continuum.

"What 'race' does is to reify these differences as deriving from some imagined natural grouping of people that does not, in fact, exist, except in our heads."[317] The mistake of attributing "racial" groups to these physical differences would be the same mistake a child would make who concluded that the only real colors were those of the eight crayons in the child's first box of crayons. (I vaguely remember thinking this when I was a child.) The child might later learn from a science class that colors exist along a continuum, or the child might see the many thousands of paint colors paint companies display in their samples. Occasionally my wife and I have agreed on a paint color that no paint company made but that could be obtained my mixing two of the colors a paint company made. The variations are infinite. People learn about the infinite range of colors from experience, but "race" theorists do not let experience interfere with their beliefs.[318]

In the United States, the error of "race" was compounded by segregation. Segregation was human engineering in an attempt to perpetuate a false idea of "race" by making static what is dynamic: put "black" people over there, out of the way, and keep them there. It was an attempt (still is) similar to putting the cloudy, rainy weather permanently in one place so we could visit it sometimes, and the sun-shiny weather some other place so we could enjoy it at will. Not even Nature could succeed at this. But ideologies have a power among humans that contradict nature and science.

We can imagine how this human engineering worked to further the idea of "race."

What would have happened, say 300 years ago before genetic science, if the ruling powers of a nation had decided that short people were biologically inferior to tall people, and that the superior tall people should not be polluted by the short ones?

To them it would have been clear that the short and the tall were two different types of people. Since there were both short and tall people among them, and people in between, a decision had to be made as to the dividing line. All males shorter than 5 feet, eight inches and all females shorter than 5 feet and one half-inch would be considered short, and the rest, tall. Children would be measured when they reached the age of twenty, and elders who had shrunk could give evidence of their former height by showing that their children were tall. To prevent pollution of the tall by the short, the short ones would be required to live in the lower elevations (which were, incidentally, prone to flooding), and the tall ones permitted to live elsewhere but not with the short ones. It was also asserted what to them was obvious, that the short ones did not need to eat as much meat as the tall ones, so flesh of any sort, including that from fowl and fish, was not permitted to be sold in the short community so that the tall could have enough to eat.

Unknown to them, the short ones contained some tall genes, and the tall ones contained some short genes. Thus, a short married couple would occasionally give birth to a tall child, and a tall married couple would occasionally give birth to a short child. When this happened, it was assumed (because they knew nothing then about genetics) that the wife had committed adultery, making the child illegitimate. Conservatives wanted to kill the child; liberals wanted the child to be assigned to the appropriate community. A compromise was reached to let the child live in the community in which he or she was born, but to prohibit the child from marrying.

A few generations later, any people visiting this nation could see for themselves that it consisted of two separate "races," one tall and one short. They lived separately from one another and must, therefore, prefer the company of their own kind. This would be as obvious to an outsider as to the residents themselves. None of them would be familiar with the history of the decision that led to this separation, as that history was never disclosed in the schools.

If, on the other hand, two groups that had previously been separate got together and intermingled, as has happened throughout the history of humans, over time they would lose their separate physical characteristics and become a new group. This does not mean that the range of different physical traits is lost and that everyone looks more alike. As we can observe, nearly every seven-foot basketball player had shorter parents and siblings. The range of physical characteristics does not significantly change, because the genes that determined them are not lost. If one group consisted of short people and the other consisted of tall people, and they intermingle, over time they will become not a group of average-height people but a group consisting of tall and short people and the full range in between.

Similarly, if one group has light skins and the other dark skins, if they intermingle they will become not a group of light-brown people, but a group consisting of light-skinned and dark-skinned people and the range in between. What will be newly created is the full range in between as well as the extremes.

But this has already happened. The people called "black" or "African American" already reflect this full range of skin coloring, including those who look "white" and those who became "white." In addition, they exhibit a full range of facial shapes and body types.

This also means that those who think racism can be eliminated by "whites" and "blacks" marrying one another and having "mixed" children are mistaken. Most "blacks" are already part "white" and many "whites" are part "black." There is no such thing as certain exceptions who are "mixed," because we are all mixed. There is no such thing as an "interracial" marriage, because there never were "races" to begin with.

Those who want to maintain the lie of "race" will always find a mental dividing line to sustain their false belief that "races" exist. What their minds create has little to do with reality.

What history and DNA analyses expose is that throughout the history of humankind different groups have combined to form new groups who then combine to form yet new groups. All of the efforts to prevent this process, by defining tribes, religions, nations and "races" to building walls and fences fail to prevent these continual re-combinations.

These re-combinations occur because individuals in one group connect to individuals in another group, seeing their commonality and finding that love does not have group boundaries. The attractiveness of one human being to another has never been limited by conceptions of "race."

PART III

OVERCOMING THE LIE

Chapter 7

What Racism Is Real?

The store clerk I mentioned in Chapter 2 was oppressed by racism. Some of that racism—obviously not all of it—was in his head.

He had warned me not to be an engineer, because, he thought, that opportunity was just for "whites." In his mind, I could be a doctor but not an engineer.

The racism that he believed would prevent me from being an engineer was far worse than any racism I would have encountered if I had continued in that direction. I began college as an engineering major seeking to obtain a degree in engineering physics. I was awarded a scholarship from The Boeing Company before I had decided to go to graduate school to study philosophy. As a part of that award, I received a free trip to the Boeing plant in Wichita. I was clearly not "white," and I was there in person, quite visible. I received a warm greeting (that is, by engineers' standards), shown the premises and told that after I graduated, I could be working there.

The visit occurred as I was seriously questioning my initial choice of a major and had already transferred from the School of Engineering to the School of Arts and Sciences. I was still planning then to major in physics. In spite of the nice reception at Boeing, my visit to the plant confirmed to me that I did not want to be an engineer. The engineers worked in a large impersonal room with no semblance of privacy, not even cubicles. (This was the late 1950's.) This not only did not appeal to me, I found it repulsive. The visit to the plant did not produce the results they had hoped for. Racism had nothing to do with it.

So the store clerk was wrong. But his words sensitized me to a common occurrence among "blacks": *some* of the racism they think they encounter is in their heads. I emphasize "some," because no one should conclude that racism is all imagined.

But this raises an ongoing question: How much racism is actually imposed from the outside and how much is incorrectly thought to be imposed from the outside?

In Chapter 3, I described my experiences during my college years. I mentioned the few incidents when racism affecting me was obvious and real. I also pointed out instances when other "blacks" believed there was racism when I did not. For example: the woman who believed her low grade in English was due to racism (Chapter 3). I was in the same class and believed I was graded fairly, in line with everyone else. My grades improved when my writing improved. This was not a case of her being more obviously "black" than me, for her skin was no darker than mine, and her features were consistent with the varied features of "whites." She imagined racism when it did not exist.

Fear of racism is another source of oppression. Fear restrains behavior unless the fears are overcome to test the feared situation.

There have been many times when I feared racism. Sometimes the fears were justified. Sometimes they were not. As I recorded in Chapter 3, for example, I waited many months before entering a barbershop next to campus for fear of being turned away. I overcame that fear and was served politely. I feared that I would not be served at a downtown restaurant. I was not. I tested the fear, and the fear was supported by what happened. I also feared that I would be turned away from the next place we went to that night. I tested the fear, and I was not turned away.

I worried about my safety when I traveled alone into the Deep South in 1965. I did not know if I could safely walk the streets of New Orleans with my blond friend who had invited me to her home to visit. We had met two years before when we were participants in a Quaker-sponsored summer program. This was just before Martin Luther King gave his 1963 "I have a dream" speech before hundreds of thousands on the steps of the Lincoln Memorial in Washington, D.C., an event she attended after we connected. The Civil Rights Act of 1964 passed a year later. "Interracial" marriage was still illegal in many states, including many in the North. I trusted her instincts and overcame my fear. We were cautious but did not hide our faces on the streets or pretend in public that we were not good friends. The trip was free of any incidents that could be attributed to racism. Our friendship continued.

Although I did not experience racism myself on that trip, I saw plenty of shocking evidence of it. In New Orleans, I took a walk alone through neighborhoods where, repeatedly, "blacks" lived in one block and "whites" lived in the next. The "white" blocks, even in the poor neighborhoods, were better cared for by the city, with better pavement and sidewalks. I learned that an all-"black" area of the city was the area most vulnerable to flooding, which occurred periodically.

Even more shocking were the tiny, broken-down unpainted shacks that were the homes of rural "blacks" in Mississippi, which I saw while traveling through on a Trailways bus. I saw many "white only" signs still posted along the highway in defiance of the Civil Rights Act. The interstate bus made a rest stop only where the "white only" signs were absent, in keeping with the new law. At the rest stop, I walked into the waiting room and saw that it was divided into a "black" area and a better-kept, more comfortable "white" area. There were no signs, but the tradition carried on. I knew my rights and seated myself in the "white" area, wondering what would happen. No one bothered me. These visible effects of racism in the Deep South were far more intense than anything I had seen before.

Had fear of racism guided me, I would not have done these things. I felt fear, but I did not act on it. I tested to see what would happen. In most cases, I discovered that my fears were unfounded. Had I not tested these fears, my life would have been more confined. My own fears would have confined me. Testing my fears opened doors that led to a richer life.

That I had such fears was due to racism. Overcoming these fears led to pleasant surprises and the discovery that racism was not as pervasive as I had feared, though its effects were obvious. When I participated in the first anti-war march on Washington in 1965 along with tens of thousands of others (officially underestimated at 25,000), nearly all of whom were "white," I felt immersed among people I liked.

These experiences and subsequent ones, including my awareness of my own fears, have led me to the view that the oppression racism causes is not only from the outside, but also internal. Fears and imagined oppression also create oppression.

The internal kind is self-negating. It would not exist if external oppression did not exist. But internal, self-negating oppression adds an additional layer of oppression on top of the actual oppression imposed from outside.

This makes oppression appear to the oppressed to be greater than it is. That appearance then feeds the fears, imagination and beliefs that feed the appearance.

The culture I saw in the "black" fraternity, which I described in Chapter 3, is replicated in many "black" communities around the nation. Although that was in the late 1950s, what I see today is not much different. "Blacks" reinforce self-negating oppression among themselves, convincing themselves without challenging one another that racism exists when perhaps it does but perhaps it does not. It is easier to accept that racism exists, without further inquiry, for that can be used as an excuse to keep oneself in one's place, a place that is familiar and less traumatic.

A consequence of self-negating oppression is that "blacks" will often internalize racism and impose racist ideology on each other. Thus, a "black" may experience racist oppression from another "black." For example, in many communities "blacks" will call other "blacks" "nigger" when it would be clear evidence of racism if a "white" used that term. But the use of "nigger" by one "black" against another "black" is racism of one "black" against another resulting from the internalization of racism and the acceptance of oppression. Another example: In many (but not all) "black" communities, "blacks" who excel at academics are criticized by other "blacks" for "acting white."[319] It is a mechanism "blacks" use against other "blacks" that helps keep them in an oppressed state.

Thus, a culture has developed that is compatible with acceptance of oppression and reinforces it. "Black" on "black" violence is one of the consequences of this culture, but the most devastating consequences are psychological. The culture exists due to acceptance, often unconscious, of its underlying premise, that "blacks" are biologically determined to be what they are. In other words, "blacks," to their detriment, have often accepted the lie of "race."

Thus, oppression of "blacks" is not only oppression from "whites" but also oppression by "blacks" against other "blacks." Racist oppression generally takes these three forms:

1. Oppression imposed from outside;
2. Self-imposed oppression resulting from fear of oppression and imagined oppression;
3. Oppression imposed from within, by the oppressed against the oppressed.

"Whites" cannot legitimately take any comfort in these phenomena. Racism initiated by or unopposed by "whites" is the initial and continuing cause of these different forms of racism. (This is illustrated at the end of this chapter.) But if all racism from "whites" disappeared today, tomorrow self-negating racism would still exist among "blacks" until they recognized it and turned against it.

Some of the opposition to overcoming the lie of "race" will come from "black" communities. Even some middle class "blacks" have developed a vested interest in "racial" identity. Among academics, courses, programs and departments have been developed to advance ideas about "black" and "African" culture. I believe these have been necessary to counteract the assumption that the only cultures worth studying are "white." But they also create a danger.

Looking back, I am glad that when I taught philosophy courses in the 1970's, I often used works by "black" and African authors. I taught ethics by pointing out that racism, sexism and war were ethical issues, and we discussed these issues in class. The "white" faculty were divided about what I was doing, since I was doing it not segregated into the Black Studies Department which developed then, but in the Philosophy Department which traditionally only studied "white" male writers. By being in the Philosophy Department and teaching what I taught, I was challenging the assumption of the supremacy of the "Western" intellectual tradition.

There was clearly a generational difference, since most of the opposition came from the older faculty members. I received tenure only after I initiated a lawsuit with the help of the American Civil Liberties Union. Almost everyone who supported me was "white," and most were "white" males.

Today, many "black," as well as feminist and other non-"white" faculty, have found refuge in universities in departments and centers devoted to "black," feminist, or other non-"white" issues. Thus, these issues remain segregated from the mainstream. This separation allows the mainstream to continue unchallenged. The salaries of the professors teaching in these segregated units are tied up with the existence of these units. It is sometimes in their economic interest to keep these units segregated where they are safe. We can expect some resistance from them to the undermining of their economic base. Some universities and professors recognize this problem and make sure that the professors teaching in these units have joint appointments in mainstream departments.

We must not lose sight of the goal, which is to include within the mainstream the views and experiences of those traditionally excluded from the mainstream. As this goal is reached, the segregated departments and centers will necessarily disappear. Reaching this goal requires overcoming the lie of "race," not supporting it.

Some other "black" economic interests too feed on racism. "Blacks" who reject their natural hair pay big bucks for wigs or hair straightening. The businesses that profit will want to retain their profits. Their customers will want to justify what they have done. The ministers of churches with "black" congregations may want to keep it that way. Politicians elected from "black" communities not only may appeal to shortsighted popular notions to get elected but also may benefit from the forces that keep the communities segregated. Even some "black" writers and journalists have based their careers on committing themselves to unbridgeable "racial" divisions, thereby reflecting the core thesis of "white" supremacists. Psychologically it is easier for many not to upset the status quo, even if that status quo means the acceptance of an inferior status.

Thus, the continued racist oppression of "blacks" cannot be correctly viewed as solely maintained by "white" racism. This social sickness has spread to the victims who often contribute to their own victimization. This means that the cure is not just up to "whites." It is a sickness that has affected everyone. We can help each other, without regard to "racial" differences, to cure ourselves.

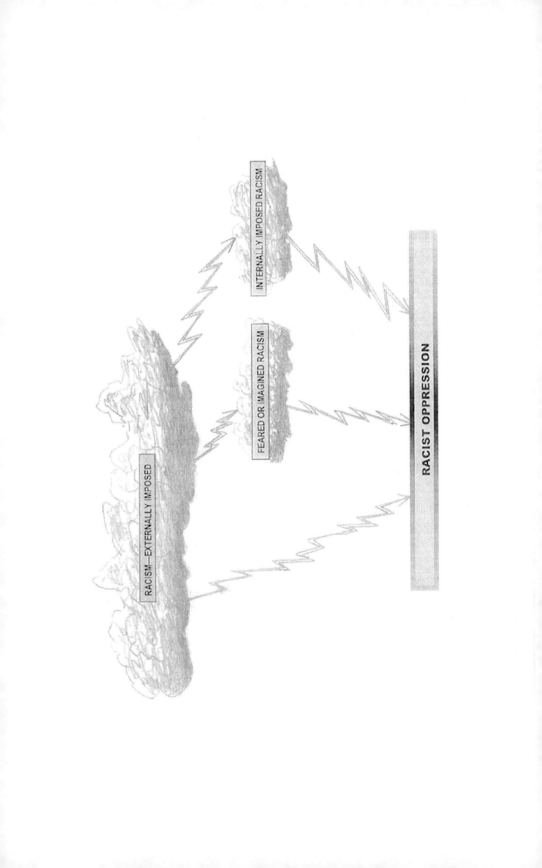

RACISM—EXTERNALLY IMPOSED

INTERNALLY IMPOSED RACISM

FEARED OR IMAGINED RACISM

RACIST OPPRESSION

Chapter 8

"Race" as Misplaced Concreteness

I was shocked as a child by something that would make an adult laugh. The incident began when my father gave me a present that I treasured.

The present was a jigsaw puzzle, the pieces of which were the 48 states. (There were only 48 then.) When put together, the result would be the United States with the 48 states clearly represented. I was probably five or six years old at the time. I learned a lot, not only about the 48 states and their locations but also about maps as well as how to put together the pieces of a jigsaw puzzle.

The funny part—from an adult standpoint—occurred when my father took me to a hill from which you could see far into the distance. I could see the Missouri river that separated Kansas from Missouri north of Kansas City, and the Kansas River that flowed into the Missouri River just as the Missouri River turned eastward into Missouri and no longer demarcated the border. The border dividing Kansas from Missouri was the state line going south of the rivers' juncture. My father pointed to where the state line was. I looked but could not see the state line. I told him I couldn't see a line. The line must be there, because I could see in on the puzzle. The states were separate and separated by lines. He laughed and said the line was imaginary. I began to cry. How could the state line not be real?

Young children often have trouble knowing what is real and what is not. Like every child, I asked about Santa Claus. My grandmother said Santa Claus was real as a symbol of Christmas. A clever answer. But to me, a symbol was not real, so I was upset.

Like symbols, state lines are real too. They determine what laws govern us. The line between Kansas and Missouri was once a line between freedom and slavery. Prior to the Civil War, "whites" fought and killed "whites" to keep Kansas a free state. But to me as a young child, the state line was not real if you could not see it on the ground.

My childish view did not understand the difference between a construct and nature. The state line is a mental construct made real by writings on paper that stated thoughts reached after discussions and compromises, and the writings became laws. It does not exist in nature.

It took a college course in philosophy to help me fully understand the difference between a construct and nature. I learned that I was not the only one to have confused the two, and that it was not just a childish error.

The error is actually a profound one. I learned about it in a course in philosophy of science taught by Dr. Peter Caws at the University of Kansas around 1960. One of his assigned texts was *Science and the Modern World* by Alfred North Whitehead.[320] Whitehead described what he called "The Fallacy of Misplaced Concreteness": "mistaking the abstract for the concrete."[321]

Whitehead explained how this fallacy is committed by the philosophy of "scientific materialism," a philosophy that assumes that reality is not what we directly experience but instead consists of bits of material that underlie what we see, moving about in accordance with mathematical laws. Whitehead pointed out that this was a confusion of assuming that a human-created mental construct, depicting reality as consisting of bits of matter moving about in space, was the true reality, and that nature as we experienced it with its colors and sensations was but an illusory product of the motion of bits of matter. Thus, if the construct is the true reality, "nature is a dull affair, soundless, scentless, colourless; merely the hurrying of material, endlessly, meaninglessly."[322]

Some scientists still commit this error, even calling a recently detected particle the "God particle,"[323] as if true reality lay in a material particle that only a few scientists could detect and not in the common reality that humans experience through their senses. This is not to say that there is an error in the scientific method, but instead to say that there is an error in assuming the postulated particles are the only true reality. After all, the postulated particles are only postulated from what humans see, such as flashes on photographs, and human interpretations of what these flashes mean. If we deny that our sense perceptions are real, then what we see is not real, so interpretations of them must also be unreal.

Thus, if what we experience though our senses is not real, we undermine the sources of information that are used to postulate the particles that cannot be directly sensed. Science requires reliance on our sense perceptions to correct errors in mental constructions. If we deny the reality of our sense perceptions, then we are thrown into a world of complete uncertainty where ideas cannot be tested except against other ideas that are postulated in human imagination without foundation. Scientists who adopt a philosophy that reality is other than what sense perception reveals are undermining science itself. Ultimately, that is Whitehead's brilliant point.

This is not to say that the particles and energy fields postulated by scientists are not *also* real. But their reality is a construct inferred from observations made through the senses. Thus, they cannot be more real than what our senses reveal. They too constitute reality to the extent that our inferences are correct. But it is only through what we sense that the correctness of this inferred reality can be tested.

Reality consists of many levels. The inferred particles of physics operate at a level that provides levers for altering the reality we live in. But these particles are inferred from experience, from what is seen, from instruments that can be handled, from writings and charts that emerge from our fingers. The fundamental reality, that upon which all else is based, is sensory experience, the sounds, scents and colors that Whitehead indicants are missing from a world of particles. Other levels of reality build upon the fundamental reality of what we directly sense as individuals.

The concept of "race" is also an inferred idea, an abstraction invented by people who called themselves scientists.

If we pay attention to what we see and directly sense when we encounter a person (as I described in the Introduction), we do not see a "race." We see a person with specific physical characteristics, a particular face with particular eyes, nose and mouth, a particular shape of the head, a particular kind of hair, a particular color of hair, a particular body shape, a particular color of skin, a particular expression, a particular voice, and so on. These particulars create a uniqueness than enables one to identify that person when seen again.

The idea that this particular person is of a particular "race" is an idea that results from taking an abstraction, a mental construct, called "race" and applying it to the multitude of characteristics that allow us to identify that person in the middle of a crowd. But we do not actually *see* the construct. We impose the construct onto what we see and use it to place what we see into various "racial" categories.

Those who have observed people from around the world or done widespread genetic testing know that the idea of "races" is wrong. Anyone can see this with his or her own eyes. The physical differences among people are along continuums, not in discrete lumps. For example, there are continuums of differences among people across Eurasia, with no sharp divisions. There are continuums of differences within America. Anyone can see these continuums by riding the many subways of Manhattan. But we can only see the continuums if we are not predisposed to see "races" instead of people.

Superimposed on the false concept of "race" are stereotypes. Stereotypes are false concepts within a false concept. Among these stereotypes is that of "black male" or "black man." According to this stereotype, a "black man" is one who has struggled with poverty, faced life-threatening violence, grown up in a troubled or broken family, and encountered significant racism from police and potential employers. If he has not been in jail or prison himself, he has relatives and friends who have. A successful "black man" is one who has experienced these difficulties and overcome them. Various media formats and publishers play on this stereotype and reinforce it.

Stereotypes are exaggerations and extensions of smaller realities. The smaller realities exist, but stereotypes crowd out other realities. Among the other realities that are crowded out are the realities of middle-class people who are designated as "black" or "African American" by social convention. They are people like me whose life experiences differ only a little from that of middle-class "white" people. We did not grow up in poverty, did not encounter violence, did not have relatives or friends who had trouble with the law or police, and had no difficulty obtaining higher education from the nation's best universities. I mention "us" in this context to illustrate the extent to which the stereotype is false.

The stereotype is so strong, however, that some will regard us as not really "black." Yet we are as "black" as those who fit the stereotype (given that "black" itself is a false construct). To say that we are not really "black" is to give the stereotype a greater reality than the individuals to whom the stereotype is applied. Those who say this commit the error of "misplaced concreteness." It is the individuals who are concrete. Stereotypes ignore individual variations.

Some will point to a significant percentage of us who benefited from having lighter skins—again implying that we are not really "black." But among us are many people with dark skins. One of my last conversations with my uncle before he died was about any racism he had experienced in Kansas City, Missouri, since his arrival there in the 1950s. He had dark skin. He said he had not encountered any racism directed personally at him. He was a state legislator and a successful business man in the "white" world of commercial real estate. This indicates that there are other factors besides skin color, factors not understood, that are involved in racist incidents.

Misplaced concreteness is not just a mental error. It is an error that affects how one lives and interacts with others. Is the other an individual, unique person or an idea of what various people are supposed to be like? To relate to others as ideas is to avoid knowing who they are.

Constructs and stereotypes about "racial" groups are barriers to communication, understanding and human connection. In 2014 an experienced editorial writer wrote critically about "white America." The writer's own statistics showed that "white America" was divided, disproving the idea that there is such a thing. I responded with a letter to the editor, which was published, pointing out that there is no such thing as "white America" or "black America."[324] Similarly, there is no such thing as "the white man" or "the black man." These are mental constructs used to oversimplify and falsify reality and cloud our perception of individual differences.

A similar construct emerges in Ta-Nehisi Coates' currently popular book, *Between the World and Me*,[325] which presents a rather blurred picture of a united and oppressive "white" world. But what the book pictures as united has always been divided. (I have indicated a few of these divisions in Chapter 4.) There have always been "white" dissenters and pioneers on the side of justice.[326] Constructs that ignore them are both false and unfair. In support of the construct, his book assumes that the "white" world democratically reflects the "white" majority,[327] but that assumption naively ignores the political power of well-financed special interests that often determine policies that may or may not be supported by a majority.[328]

Constructs by themselves do not cause racism. However, racism is supported, often inadvertently, by people who accept the constructs. The constructs also create barriers to uniting people across "racial" divisions. These barriers impede the creation of the coalitions needed to effect beneficial social change.

Racism is the product of ingrained and institutionalized ways of thinking and behavior that individuals participate in (or not) in varying degrees. The individuals who participate unconsciously, who include "whites," "blacks" and others, can be made aware of their participation. When made aware, many will find ways to turn against racism instead of supporting it.[329] We become blind to the process of change initiated by individuals if we think of the problem in terms of constructs that override our individuality.

To think of people primarily in terms of their "races" is to commit the same error that I committed when I thought that state lines were actual lines of nature marked on the ground. It is to confuse a construct with nature. In reality, each of us is a unique individual. As unique individuals, we are not marked with "race." "Race" is a construct that we impose on what we see. To see the reality of unique individuals is to overcome the fallacy of misplaced concreteness. It is an essential step we must take to overcome the lie of "race."

Chapter 9

Understanding Merit and the Need to Replace "Affirmative Action"

Affirmative action in academia was designed in a way that, intentionally or not, preserves the myth of "white" male mental superiority. The social objective of achieving diversity is a laudatory one, but affirmative action has been another way of giving "blacks"—and women—an inferior intellectual status. It is a way of viewing "blacks" and women as intellectually needy and affirmative action as a mental welfare benefit handed out in the interest of fairness. The myth is fed by admission criteria that have defined cognitive skills too narrowly.

Overall, affirmative action was a well-intentioned and mostly successful effort to counteract ingrained discrimination. Its success, however, came at a cost. The cost was the preservation of the accepted idea that "blacks," women and others whom affirmative action benefited were nonetheless intellectually not as worthy as "white" males. The cost was also the perception that individual "whites," particularly but not always men, were being discriminated against to attain social and political goals. In some cases the perception had a basis in reality. But overall, the cost was to preserve a two-tiered population in which "whites," particularly "white" males, occupied the tier considered to contain the most qualified.

In spite of its costs, the nation has benefited from affirmative action. My criticism is in the interest of moving forward to something better, not to regret the past. It is now time to correct the negatives of affirmative action, not by returning to the past but by developing a fairer and more realistic conception of merit.

To move forward, we first need to appreciate why affirmative action was necessary. The history of affirmative action (well described in Terry Anderson's book, *The Pursuit of Fairness: A History of Affirmative Action*)[330] reveals that early governmental efforts to eliminate "racial" and gender discrimination generally failed. The promise of equality, advanced by the critically important Civil Rights Act of 1964 and, for women, the Equal Pay Act of 1963, was not met. Built-in methods that favored "white" males were too entrenched to be altered by laws requiring equal treatment.

Urban riots followed. The United States, calling itself the leader of the "free world," again got a red face. "Civil rights reform came to be seen as crucial to U.S. foreign relations."[331] Something had to be done to reaffirm the standing of the United States in the world. "Fires in the streets contributed to a shift in the [President] Johnson administration's policy."[332] Affirmative action, originally presented by President John F. Kennedy as affirmative action to end discrimination, morphed into affirmative action to bring "blacks" particularly (since they were the rioters) into the workforce in proportion to their numbers in the general population. "White" women did not riot (at least not violently in visible groups), but they succeeded in being included in many affirmative action plans, though this took longer, for initially the legitimate claims of women were ignored and belittled.[333]

These affirmative action programs as they further developed in the 1970s could correctly be characterized as giving preferences to those who were not "white" males. But preferences were (and are) preferences in the context of narrow criteria that determine merit, criteria that favored (and often still favor) "white" males, particularly middle and upper class "white" males who have had the benefits of a decent education. Given these ingrained and largely unseen customary preferences given to "white" males, it is not obvious that the preferences given to those who were not "white" males actually resulted in any significant unfairness, except perhaps in a few individual cases.

Because affirmative action programs did not address the concept of merit, but instead divided the population into "white" males accepted on merit and the others with less merit but having a plus factor for social justice or diversity, the underlying acceptance of the assumption of "white" male intellectual superiority was not noticed and not examined. If anything, the affirmative action programs reinforced that assumption. "Blacks" and "white" women accepted these programs, because they gained from them, as did the nation.

But in being bought off by these benefits, they typically did not question the underlying assumption that the "white" males who qualified were as a group more qualified than the rest. The problem lies in the defining of "qualifications."

In higher education, the bias favoring "white" males—more specifically, upper-class and middle-class "white" males with well-educated parents—is the result of over-reliance on standardized test scores. As I will explain, test scores reflect on a certain kind of intelligence, a narrow kind that does not necessarily translate into accomplishments in the real world.

Standardized tests are taken in an artificial environment, a room that is isolated from the rest of the world. The questions to be answered are relatively short, unlike problems in the real world. Most of all, there is only one correct answer for each question (even if the correct answer is "all of the above"). This too does not reflect the real world, where correct answers are frequently not knowable at the time a decision has to be made and where reasonable people can disagree.

The testing environment and tests themselves not only are artificial, they also represent a narrow world where correct answers are knowable and can be discerned from a short scenario. This narrow world has only a marginal bearing on the real world, where trial and error and risk-taking are required to solve real problems, and where tolerance of alternative approaches is an admirable quality that may lead to productive compromises. The idea of compromising to get a workable result cannot be tested with questions that have only one correct answer.

In addition, the standardized test cannot test the ability to achieve results that can only be achieved through teamwork and cooperation. The standardized test is an affair involving only each individual functioning in isolation from others. The real world is an affair mostly requiring interaction with others.

Throughout my life and careers, I have had to work with others to get desired results. Even when I worked alone to discern the meaning of a complicated regulatory text, I had to explain my findings to others and consider any feedback or disagreement. The standardized test might reflect my ability to do the former but not the ability to do the latter. Without the latter—the interaction with others—my findings would have no impact on the real world.

I have no personal ax to grind here. I usually scored well on standardized tests. Tom also scored well, which I knew because we sometimes appeared in the same honors classes. These tests were not an impediment for me but a way to open doors. But, as you can see from Part I, my intellectual background differed little from that of middle-class "white" males with well-educated parents. The same was true for Tom. Reliance on these tests created a bias that favored people like me. My son also benefited from these tests. The tests created a form of affirmative action for those with educated parents.

Sheryll Cashin has advanced the idea of "place not race" for college admissions.[334] She argues for eliminating consideration of "race" in affirmative action programs and instead for giving special consideration to those from impoverished backgrounds and those who have overcome adversity. I partially agree. Cashin and I are pointing in a similar direction, but there are important differences.

She states, for example, that "noncognitive traits—like resilience, self-control, and the ability to delay gratification and persist past disappointments and failures—are more critical to ultimate success than cognitive skills."[335] While this may be true, my point is that high scores on standardized tests to not adequately reflect "cognitive" skills.

Cognitive skills include the ability to detect uncertainty, the creation and evaluation of a reasonable course of action given uncertainty, and the ability to engage in intellectual exchanges with others in a manner that leads to arriving at views that would not have been arrived at if the exchanges had not occurred. These are not tested in standardized tests. Only a small portion of cognitive skills is tested in these tests. Thus, equating test scores with cognitive ability is wrong. In addition to noncognitive skills, we need to look for cognitive skills that standardized tests do not test.

In addition, Cashin's book does not clearly take us beyond those existing programs that set aside a major portion of the admissions to be determined by test scores and another portion to be determined by "noncognitive" factors. In the book's conclusion she states, "One first step would be to base affirmative action upon structural disadvantage, not race."[336] This step misses something critical.

To improve higher education, we have to redefine the meaning of "merit" and what it means to be "qualified." If this is done correctly, no "affirmative action" or similar program by another name will be needed.

Even if test scores are considered in college admissions, they should be treated not as a measure of intelligence but as a partial indicator of intellectual growth and, thus, the potential for further intellectual growth.

But to measure a person's intellectual growth, we have to take into consideration that person's starting point. An applicant who grew up in a stable, middle-class household, had college-educated professional parents, went to a high quality high school, and had only a slightly above-average score on the test for college admission did not have much intellectual growth on the matters tested. An applicant (of any "race") who grew up in an unstable, impoverished household, had parents who were not college-educated, and went to an academically deficient school and had the same slightly above-average score on the test for college admission would show very significant intellectual growth on the matters tested. Although their test scores were the same, the second applicant's intellectual growth was significantly greater than the first applicant's.

But more importantly, we have to acknowledge that the tests test only a narrow range of skills and not the full range of skills needed for success in academia or the world.

A more insidious effect of measuring merit based on test scores is the effect these scores have on expectations. "The academic expectations of teachers and parents, educational institutions, and society at large can shape children's lives in school and beyond through self-fulfilling prophecies."[337] In general (there are always exceptions), those who had lower scores would be expected to perform at a lower level than those with higher scores. If some were thought to have been given preference due to affirmative action, they would be visible as those who were not "white" males.

Teachers who accepted that tests measured merit would logically expect more of those students who were not given preferences to gain admission, namely their "white" male students. These teachers would generally assume that these "white" males were more qualified and would encourage them accordingly. Students who accepted that tests measured merit would logically expect less of themselves if they believed that their test scores were below the average of those admitted. They also would be more likely to doubt their ability to succeed if faced with teachers and classmates who also doubted their ability to succeed.

In these ways the test scores give those with higher scores a higher level of confidence in their ability to succeed, and those who score lower a lower level of confidence in this ability. That difference in confidence can lead to actual differences in accomplishments. Yet, these differences are encouraged by the belief that the test scores actually adequately measure things that are of critical importance, things called "merit" and "qualifications."[338]

It is a false belief that they do. In my work as a lawyer for a state health and human services agency, I faced real-world tasks. I supervised a handful of other lawyers and participated with others in the process of hiring them. I am pleased to say that our hiring efforts were usually quite successful. *Rarely did we take test scores or law school grades into consideration.* There was a reason for this. The qualities we were looking for would not have been reflected in those items.

These are some of the main qualities we wanted and successfully obtained in the lawyers we hired:

- Ability to see the strengths as well as the weaknesses of an opponent's argument.
- Ability to present facts objectively even if some of them support an opposing view.
- Ability to write a lengthy persuasive and well-organized argument (requiring 10 to 20 pages) without excessive verbiage and within court-ordered page limits.
- Ability to be poised and persuasive when presenting an oral argument in court while maintaining respect for the judicial context.
- Ability to discern the essential issues contained in a file of documents that may consist of several hundred pages.
- Ability to interact with colleagues in a way that is respectful while expressing disagreements and engaging in dialogue when appropriate.
- A sense of fairness and integrity. Since we were employed in a state agency working in the public interest, it was important to have a sense of when the agency might be considering actions that were not in the public interest or extending its power inappropriately, and to be able and willing to lead others away from considering any approach that would be unfair.
- Acceptance of the agency's mission statement that included providing quality health care to people in need.

I know of no standardized test or law school examination that would establish that a person has these qualities or the ability and desire to develop them.

The qualities that we did look for were qualities that would enable the agency to fulfill its mission. Similarly, universities and colleges (as well as employers) should look for and develop the qualities that are in accordance with their missions. Typically there is little or no connection between the missions of an institution and standardized tests used to screen applicants.

Here is a small selection from university mission statements quoted from the universities' websites in December, 2014. (There is no suggestion here that these universities are not fulfilling their missions or that they do not have diverse campuses. All of these universities express a commitment to diversity.)

Cornell University	Cornell's mission is to discover, preserve, and disseminate knowledge; produce creative work; and promote a culture of broad inquiry throughout and beyond the Cornell community. Cornell also aims, through public service, to enhance the lives and livelihoods of our students, the people of New York, and others around the world.
Emory University	Emory University's mission is to create, preserve, teach, and apply knowledge in the service of humanity.
Harvard Law School (Harvard University)	To educate leaders who contribute to the advancement of justice and the well being of society.
UCLA	UCLA's primary purpose as a public research university is the creation, dissemination, preservation and application of knowledge for the betterment of our global society. . . . UCLA advances knowledge, addresses pressing societal needs and creates a university enriched by diverse perspectives where all individuals can flourish. . . .
University of Florida	Our mission is to enable our students to lead and influence the next generation and beyond for economic, cultural and societal benefit. . . .
University of Michigan	The mission of the University of Michigan is to serve the people of Michigan and the world through preeminence in creating, communicating, preserving

	and applying knowledge, art, and academic values, and in developing leaders and citizens who will challenge the present and enrich the future.
University of Texas, Austin	The mission of The University of Texas at Austin is to achieve excellence in the interrelated areas of undergraduate education, graduate education, research and public service. . . . The university contributes to the advancement of society through research, creative activity, scholarly inquiry and the development of new knowledge. The university preserves and promotes the arts, benefits the state's economy, serves the citizens through public programs and provides other public service.
University of Wisconsin, Madison	. . . The primary purpose of the University of Wisconsin–Madison is to provide a learning environment in which faculty, staff and students can discover, examine critically, preserve and transmit the knowledge, wisdom and values that will help ensure the survival of this and future generations and improve the quality of life for all. . . .

A common element in all of these mission statements is the goal of improving society or humanity. What does this have to do with scores on standardized tests?

A person could get a perfect score on standardized tests and have no desire to improve society or humanity. This is not to say that the desire to improve society or humanity is necessary for college admission, but that it should be taken into consideration for those colleges and universities that make this a part of their mission statements. By taking this into consideration, the school would be acknowledging a qualification of the applicant, not an additional factor to be considered separate from qualifications.

Another qualification to be considered is an applicant's ability to overcome adversity. This is where the qualities Sheryl Cashin describes become relevant, among them "resilience, self-control, and the ability to delay gratification and persist past disappointments and failures."[339] These qualities are not separate from an applicant's qualifications but an integral part of them.

Now we have to be careful to make an important distinction which can easily be ignored or distorted by the opponents of diversity. Among the adversities that an applicant may have overcome is "racial" discrimination. An applicant who has faced significant "racial" discrimination and succeeded in spite of it has a quality of overcoming adversity that adds to that applicant's qualifications.

This is not the same as taking into consideration the applicant's "race." For example, not all "African Americans" have faced significant "racial" discrimination. I experienced "racial" discrimination as I described in Part I, but not enough to create much of a barrier to overcome. Had my skin been considerably darker, or had I lived as a child in a more conservative city, my experiences may have been different and my life may have been more difficult. Many and probably most "African Americans" have experienced significant adversity in the form of "racial" discrimination. Overcoming such adversity should be considered along with overcoming other kinds of adversity, such as poverty, parents without college degrees, lack of access to good schools, and broken homes.

What is being considered here is not an applicant's "race" but the perception of the applicant's "race" by others who, based on such perception, discriminated against the applicant in ascertainable ways. If the applicant suffered significantly from such discrimination, that discrimination should be considered among the adversities the applicant faced. To not take this adversity into consideration is to discriminate against the applicants who have faced and overcome adversity.

The hiring practices of a very successful company, Google, take into consideration whether a job applicant has had "to develop a greater degree of grit and determination in the face of difficult personal circumstances."[340] There is no reason why colleges and universities should not do the same for admissions.

For a college or university to fulfill its mission, it needs to admit students who are projected to help it to do so. The school needs to figure out what qualifications a student needs to accomplish this. There should be no separate program, called "affirmative action" or any other name, to consider factors that are not qualifications. Such programs create two classes of citizenship within the school: those who are admitted without such programs and those who are admitted only because of such programs. The existence of such programs gives the former a higher intellectual standing and the latter a lower intellectual standing. Instead of creating diversity, such programs divide the student body into the intellectual haves and have-nots. They perpetuate "racial" bias and, accordingly, should be abolished.

The school needs to examine whether scores on standardized tests have any bearing whatsoever on its mission. The burden is on the school to establish such a bearing. (The same principle applies to employers.) If it cannot carry that burden, the test scores are nothing more than an irrelevant screening device which historically has served to favor the privileged, thereby enhancing the inequality that already exists in what is supposed to be a democratic society.

If the school does not take into consideration the adversity an applicant has overcome, the school is discriminating against that applicant and unfairly favoring those who have already been favored. Even if test scores can be connected to a university's mission, they should be evaluated in the context of the circumstances of the applicant to locate those who may not have the highest test scores but who scored well and also have developed "grit and determination in the face of difficult personal circumstances."

What I am proposing here implies a complete revamping of the process for determining admissions to institutions of higher learning. But "there are strong political and ideological forces that keep the system as it is."[341] Nonetheless, some colleges and universities are making appropriate changes.[342]

The outcome of testing to determine college admissions is the preservation of privilege. The purpose of traditional affirmative action is to add visual diversity to privilege without challenging privilege.

The system as it is strengthens the privileged and undermines the values underlying democracy. Those values recognize the equal worth of every human being. When properly implemented these values lead to social structures and processes that support individual efforts to attain self-fulfillment. The efforts that are supported should not be limited to those of a privileged elite.[343]

In general, standardized tests have little to do with the qualities needed for real-world accomplishments. Their narrow focus benefits those who already have had the benefits of educated parents and a supportive environment. These tests have created affirmative action for this privileged elite. By broadening the conception of qualifications and merit, we can safely eliminate affirmative action for any special group and place all on an equal footing.

Chapter 10

On Being a Person

What is my identity?

Clearly, from what I have said here, I cannot identify myself by "race." "Races" do not exist except as a socially and politically created historical lie. I will not identify myself in those false terms.

Some people will say I am "black," because society defines me as "black." But, as I will explain, my identity does not depend on how others define me.

Perhaps, I can identify myself by ethnicity. Being an "African American" would then identify my ethnicity, not my "race." But there are big problems with this, as I will explain.

First, I need to clarify the difference between "race" and ethnicity. The two concepts are often confused and blended into one another.

"Race" is about biology. Ethnicity is about culture. Culture is not biologically determined. We have to think of ethnicity free of "racial" thinking if we are to understand ethnicity.

Culture in this sense "refers to the sum total of life patterns passed on from one generation to another with a group of people." It includes "institutions, language, values, religious ideals, habits of thinking, artistic expressions, and patterns of social and interpersonal relationships."[344] An ethnicity is an identifiable culture.

Cultures can be observed and described. There are no biological determinants of culture. A person born and growing up in one culture can assimilate into another culture. This phenomenon too is observable.

Thus, a person is not determined to be any particular way as a necessary consequence of growing up in a particular culture. While people are taught the values, thinking habits, and patterns of social interaction of the culture in which they grew up, they can change and adopt a different way of living. Ethnicity is a matter of choice whereas one's supposed "race" is not. One can choose to "fit in" with the cultural group he or she grew up in, or not fit in, or leave and merge into an elsewhere.

We see this constantly. I remember once I was seated in a crowded bus in Boston, reading and not paying attention to those around me, when the irritating voices of three older teenage girls penetrated my consciousness. They were standing in front of me, engaged in animated conversation, all sounding alike and saying "like" and "you know" like in every other word. I looked up and saw two blond-haired girls and a third whose ancestry appeared to be from Asia, probably China. The third was just as American as the other two (and just as irritating). They dressed alike too. In urban areas today, there is nothing unusual about this. (As I explained in Chapter 6, that we can often determine a person's geographical ancestry from his or her appearance has nothing to do with "race.") The girl whose ancestry was from Asia chose to be an American. As far as I could tell, she had succeeded.

Also, every cultural group seems to have its misfits. They may choose to suffer, become leaders, or leave to find a more congenial place.

Of course, there are places in the world where such choice is extremely difficult. But there is always a choice, even to risk one's own life.

One problem I have with defining my ethnicity is that I grew up with a multiplicity of cultural influences, as is typical of everyone. Here are a few of them.

I was born and grew up in the United States. That makes me an American. (Yet, I would rather live in Europe than in Florida.)

I was born and grew up in Kansas. That makes me a Midwesterner—sort of. Shortly after becoming an adult, I left and never returned to the Midwest except for short visits.

I have lived just over half of my life in New England (including four years in graduate school in New Haven). Before settling in New England permanently in 1980, I lived fourteen years on the West Coast: three in Seattle and the remainder in Berkeley and San Francisco. I feel most "at home" in New England.

I grew up outside of the Confederacy, in the culture of the North, not the South.

I grew up speaking English. I have no direct experience with those who grew up with another primary language or in a bilingual setting.

I grew up in an urban area. I know nothing about rural life.

I grew up in a stable middle-class environment. I have been middle-class all of my life. I have no direct experience of poverty or extreme wealth.

I am a male. I know little or nothing of what it would have been like to have grown up as a woman.

My parents were college-educated as were most of my relatives of my parents' generation and many of my relatives of my grandparents' generation.

My parents and paternal grandfather were scientists and science teachers.

Some of my most treasured experiences since moving to the Boston area thirty-five years ago have occurred when sitting in Symphony Hall and listening to the Boston Symphony perform music of Beethoven, Mahler, Bruckner or Brahms, or certain pieces of other classical composers. To that I would add sitting in Fenway Park with my son when he was a child and watching the Red Sox.

I am what is called an "African-American."

All of these factors constituted cultural influences and contributed to the shaping of my environment. Why should being an "African American" be any more important (or less important) than these other cultural influences. (I doubt that I have named or even recognized all of the important ones.) I believe all of those I have mentioned are no less important than being an "African American." My ethnicity is a conglomeration of all of these (and other) cultural factors. To identify myself as an "African American" is to ignore all of the other factors that are part of my blended culture.

Also, to identify my ethnicity as "African American" would suggest that I have more in common with other "African Americans" than with those who are not "African Americans." That suggestion would be false.

I remember my reaction when I read James Baldwin's *Another Country* in graduate school (not a part of course work). The novel was about people who were not familiar to me, about a culture I had never known. Yet, it was about "African Americans" and written by an "African American." I was fascinated by the book much in the same way that I was fascinated by anthropological studies of cultures I knew nothing about. I can say the same about Toni Morrison's *Song of Solomon* and many other books by "African Americans" about "African Americans."

In the summer of 1965 I participated in a program that brought college students from the North to teach courses in "black" colleges in the South. In my group of about ten or so teachers, two were "black" (including me). I had much more in common with the other teachers in this group than I had with the students or administrators at the college. The cultural division was not between "black" and "white" but between North and South.

Is there something odd about an African American who does not like gospel music? The Baptist church I most frequently attended as a child was like many northern urban "black" Baptist churches during those times, which did not accept gospel music.[345] I rarely heard this kind of music as a child and I have never liked it. (I like blues and jazz—whether performed by "blacks," "whites," or others.)

Perhaps my identity is that of sharing a common oppression with other "African Americans." But we do not all share a common oppression. The experiences of northern middle-class "blacks" and southern impoverished rural "blacks" are remarkably different. The degree of oppression a "black" person experiences is related not only to class, education and location but also to skin color. In addition, I seek identity in the overcoming of suffering, not in suffering. Suffering in common with others has no appeal to me. I see nothing honorable about it.

Thus, there are many ways in which the "ethnicity" of "African Americans" is too diverse and too blended with other influences to be described or defined. The varied experiences of the "African American" middle class are not widely known and are far from any stereotypes. A piece of this experience is described in a book about my great uncle: *Luther P. Jackson and a Life for Civil Rights.*[346] My grandparents and most of their brothers and sisters were middle class; their children even more so.

Perhaps, then, my ethnicity is simply that of a middle-class American? But this does not work either. When I travel to Europe, I feel quite comfortable in urban European environments: London, Berlin, Madrid, Budapest, Zagreb, Lisbon. When I traveled recently to northern Florida, I felt that I was in an alien environment and could not wait to leave.

From my experiences and my travels, I believe that my ethnicity— that is, the cultural group I feel most comfortable with—would be described as college-educated middle-class professionals, writers and artists who are politically left of center and not bound to any particular ideology. They consist of men and women of many nationalities with skins of all shades. Within this group it does not matter whether you are "white," "black," yellow, or red, or gay or "straight." This group is defined by its values. It has no common ideology except that of fairness and respect for others. Its location is interspersed throughout other locations. It should remain nameless, because names attach to static things, and this cultural group is fluid. The idea of "group" is not even appropriate.

But something is still missing.

Ethnicity is not a matter of vanilla or chocolate. It is not even a matter of adding more individual flavors. If ethnicity were ice cream, my ethnicity, like most people's ethnicities, would consist of a swirl of multiple flavors that meld together.

But as for my identity, even multiple swirl leaves something out. Let's imagine my identity somewhat like ice cream swirled with many flavors: vanilla, chocolate, strawberry, lemon, banana, coconut, pineapple, and so on. These flavors would be like the many cultural influences I have described.

What would multiple swirl taste like? You cannot know without actually tasting it. You have to have a scoop of it sitting in a cup in your hand, a spoon to lift some to your mouth, and then you savor what it is.

What you would be tasting is the particular ice cream in the cup in your hand. The identity of that ice cream is not just multiple swirl, it is what it tastes like to you at that time.

Something similar defines my identity. I am who I am, an individual person to be experienced in my uniqueness. I am not merely the confluence of multiple cultures. I am not my ethnicity, however defined. The cultures that influence me constitute the background from which I emerge as a unique person.

Just as I see myself as unique, so do I see others.

This is not to say that my individuality is isolated from that of others. It is not. In my view, my identity as an individual includes supporting others in their efforts to be individuals. This is a social, not an anti-social, process.

Others are important. But as an individual, I choose how I connect with others. I feel that it is important to see myself in relation to others, to history, to ideas, but I am the one who determines what that relationship is or will be. My "community" is how I define it. It is not some pre-determined construct like nation, ethnicity, class, or "race."

These constructs are socially pre-defined and imposed from outside of ourselves. Whether we allow them to define us is up to each of us. We do not have to accept what society provides, particularly if what society provides is based on myths or lies. No one has to accept what is assumed in the cultural environment. Recognizing this is what it means to have an identity as an individual. As an individual, anyone can choose whether to accept a predefined "racial" identity or to ignore it. Ignoring it means that who you are is not determined by what others think.

Asserting one's individuality in the face of social pressures is not an easy task. In varying degrees, everyone compromises with social pressures. No one gets 100% free of them. It is a continual process of discovery to determine "who am I" in the midst of others saying you are x or y. Assisting others to engage in this process is a valuable form of human connection and a way of creating a new community.

Although it is a matter of personal choice to identify with socially pre-defined groups, it is a choice fraught with peril. Seeking identity with a group may channel us to take less responsibility for our own lives and shift that responsibility to the group we identify with or to another group perceived to be in opposition to our own group. It is always tempting to blame the oppositional group for our problems. But this approach to living avoids personal responsibility.

The kind of human beings we are—loving, hateful, spiteful, kind, resentful, affirming—is what we individually chose to be regardless of our circumstances or membership in any conceivable group. In this sense we, as individuals, are responsible for who we are regardless of what group we might consider ourselves to be a part of.

"Race" consciousness simply gets in the way of discovering who we are and who others are as individuals. Those who identify themselves by "race" or "ethnicity" may be creating a self-imposed wall that stands in the way of seeing who they themselves are and who others are as separate, unique people. It is a form of "misplaced concreteness" to see others merely in terms of our conceptualizations of them.

Identity begins with being oneself and being aware of oneself. To seek oneself in group identity is to risk losing awareness of who we are and who others are. When that awareness is lost, we become people who relate to others in terms of the categories we place them into, blocking our ability to see and love who they are in their individual uniqueness.

The concreteness of humanity, thus, is the individual. The individual is the fundamental human reality. All other levels of reality build upon it. The core of our individuality is a combination of what we experience and the decisions we make.

But the individual is more than one's self. Just as who we are as individuals is our fundamental reality, so we must recognize that the individual is also the fundamental reality of others. Our reality as individuals is anchored in our connection to other individuals if, that is, others are experienced *as* individuals and not as some combination of abstractions or constructs.

Our connections to other individuals begins with the awareness of those who are most important to us: partners, lovers, children and parents, for example, who would wrench our hearts out if they died unexpectedly. Add to these experiences our sensory experiences of beauty and taste, whether the beauty of a work of art, a formation of clouds, a flower blooming, a magnificent old tree, the taste of fruit, the warmth, scent and taste of a child, partner or lover. Also add our experiences of suffering and pain, especially when they are the outcome of a connection lost. These are experiences that we have as individuals, alone but for our connection to others who so similarly have experiences like our own.

This fundamental reality I have become increasingly aware of with age. I reflect on past experiences and more deeply experience present ones. I am happy that the false reality of "race"—a reality on the level with other realities of lies, myths and unfounded beliefs that also impinge on our lives—did not interfere with my connection to others. Had it done so, it would have been a great loss.

Chapter 11

Encouraging the Future

Every solution to the problem of racism in our society must begin with the explicit realization that human "races" do not exist. If we are to eliminate racism, we must rid ourselves of the very idea of "race."

"Races" were invented and sustained for the primary purpose of ranking groups of people hierarchically. As long as we think and talk in terms of "races," we will perpetuate this ranking. Well-intended efforts to say that all "races" are equal only reinforce the concept of "race" used by others who insist on hierarchy.

Often those who oppose racism, including victims of racism, accept the very concept of "race" that racists have historically relied on to support their views. When the victims and opponents of racism accept and affirm the concept of "race," they unwittingly support the very racism they oppose.

We cannot have democracy based on the idea of human equality and also have "races" subject to hierarchical ranking.

It is one thing to talk about the problem. It is another to do something about it. To the extent that we accept the values of democracy[347] and treasure human diversity, we must act.

The first step is to change the way we see and think. I have discussed part of this process in the Introduction. This is not about changing someone else. It is not about looking for someone to take the lead. It is about what each of us can do. It is about changing our own mental habits.

Once we make it a mental habit to see the many different ways in which people differ physically from one another, we will be surprised at how skin color loses its special place. This mental step is a necessary but not a sufficient one towards eliminating the false concept of "race."

The next step is to build on the first step by changing the way we talk and write. We have to find a way to talk about false ideas without reaffirming them. Every time we say "white," "black," or "African American," or talk about "race," we are affirming that "races" exist—unless, that is, we make it clear that we are using these terms to refer to the false concepts that people believe.

In writing, I have chosen to put "racial" terms in quotation marks to indicate that these terms refer to what people falsely think. Perhaps there is a better solution. Sometimes these terms could be preceded with "so-called" or words to that effect, whether in writing or conversation.

Another step is to recognize our individual diversity and uniqueness stripped of ethnic or "racial" identifiers. As I stated in the Preface, no one should assume that my experiences invalidate anyone else's. For example, someone else may have experienced racism where I did not. It does not follow that one of us is wrong. The idea that "race" or ethnicity creates a commonality of experience is greatly exaggerated and often wrong. To assume such commonality is to think in terms of stereotypes that are barriers to personal connection.

Finally, we must not be silent when confronted with others' acceptance or affirmance of "racial" thinking. We must persistently tell the news media to stop using "racial" terms without recognition of their falseness. We must question those who want to affirm that "race" is real, even when the victims of racism affirm it. Silence is racism's best friend.

These are actions with political consequences. Overcoming "racial" thinking will enable us to join together, without regard to "race," to overcome the lies that plague us. Supporters of the past will, as they have done before, seek to divide us to weaken us.

But overcoming "racial" thinking does not mean to forget the tremendous harm "racial" thinking has caused. While moving forward, we must fully acknowledge the past. Museums and memorials acknowledging "African-American" history, for example, should remain in place, for they acknowledge and reflect a past that is real. As we seek to move beyond that past, from lies to knowledge and inquiry, we must continually affirm that the lies were (and still are) an integral part of the fabric of American history and culture. The lies were real, affecting how everyone lived and polluting our current society. "African-American" history, however, should not convey the idea that the ancestry of all "African Americans" is mostly or entirely African, for doing so would perpetuate a lie.

While we combat racism, it is important to bear in mind that racism is a reflection of ancient and persistent ways of thinking that advocate hierarchical domination of some people by others. "Racism" is a name for only one form of this domination. Other forms include the little-acknowledged class structure of American society, a structure that keeps the poor in "their place."[348] The goal is to rise above all forms of this hierarchical way of thinking. The goal, individually and as a society, is to affirm our common and equal humanity and recognize the uniqueness of each individual—and to transform this affirmation into effective social and political action that changes our society and remedies the tragic harms of the past.

Eliminating ages of "race" consciousness will not be easy. Neither will creating a true democracy, which has not yet been accomplished.[349] The two efforts go hand in hand.

ACKNOWLEDGMENTS

Over many decades, numerous people have contributed to the experiences that made this book possible. They include friends, family, teachers, colleagues and ancestors. I could not possibly name them all, so I will not try. I thank Barbara Mende for her editing assistance. I thank my wife for her constant companionship and love. I thank my son for the enrichment that he has brought to our lives.

NOTES

BIBLIOGRAPHY

INDEX

NOTES

PREFACE

¹ Jacqueline Jones, *A Dreadful Deceit: The Myth of Race from the Colonial Era to Obama's America* (New York: Basic Books, 2013) p. xi.

INTRODUCTION

² "SJC's new rule on witnesses should help ensure justice," *The Boston Globe*, January 14, 2015, p. A10.

³ "Live together, vote together," *The Economist*, Nov. 22, 2014, p. 29.

⁴ "Voting with your wallet," *The Economist*, Sept. 13, 2014, p. 38.

⁵ "On racial issues, America is divided both black and white and red and blue," *Washington Post*, online December 26, 2014: http://www.washingtonpost.com/politics/on-racial-issues-america-is-divided-both-black-and-white-and-red-and-blue/2014/12/26/3d2964c8-8d12-11e4-a085-34e9b9f09a58_story.html?hpid=z4 .

⁶ George M. Fredrickson, *Racism: A Short History* (Princeton, New Jersey: Princeton Univ. Press, 2002), p. 156.

⁷ Ibid., p. 52.

⁸ *The Economist,* "Their own worst enemy," Nov. 7, 2015, p. 79.

⁹ The indigenous peoples of America did not all become U.S. citizens until 1926. Wendell H. Oswalt, *This Land Was Theirs: A Study of the North American Indian* (New York: John Wiley & Sons, 1966), p. 498. Even so, in 1938 seven states did not allow them to vote. Ibid., p. 499. In Canada, the indigenous peoples were not treated as citizens until 1951. Ibid., p. 498. In the Pacific Northwest towards the end of the nineteenth century, Chinese immigrants were brutally murdered. Racism against Chinese was virulent. See Kelli Estes, *The Girl Who Wrote in Silk* (Naperville, Illinois: Sourcebooks, 2015), esp. pp. 381 ff. Of course, this is less that the tip of the iceberg.

¹⁰ Ibid., p. 101.

[11] Terry H. Anderson, *The Pursuit of Fairness: A History of Affirmative Action* (New York: Oxford Univ. Press, 2004).

[12] Charles E. Silberman, *Crisis in Black and White* (New York: Vintage Books, 1964), p. 6.

[13] "Civil-war memorials: Too big to veil," *The Economist*, July 25, 2015, p. 24.

[14] See generally Peggy Pascoe, *What Comes Naturally: Miscegenation Law and the Making of Race in America* (New York: Oxford Univ. Press, 2009).

[15] *Pace v. Alabama*, 106 U.S. 583 (1883)—U.S. Supreme Court decision upholding Alabama's laws against cross-"race" marriages that equally punished both partners.

[16] Ibid. See William Lynwood Montell, *The Saga of Coe Ridge* (Knoxville: Univ. of Tennessee Press, 1970), pp. 123 ff.

[17] Winthrop Jordan, *White Over Black: American Attitudes Toward the Negro, 1550-1812* (Baltimore: Penguin Books, 1969), pp. 346-48; Julie Winch, *Between Slavery and Freedom* (Lanham, Maryland: Rowland & Littlefield, 2014), p. 88.

CHAPTER 1

[18] Written by Oscar Hammerstein II based on a novel by Edna Ferber with music by Jerome Kern.

[19] Charles Darwin, *The Descent of Man* (London: Penguin Books, 2004), Chapter 7.

CHAPTER 3

[20] William Frank Zornow, *Kansas: A History of the Jayhawk State* (Norman: Univ. of Oklahoma Press, 1957), pp. 67 ff, 84, 86, 88.

[21] The common ground is described in three of my writings to date: *Cultural Bases of Racism and Group Oppression: An Examination of Traditional "Western" Concepts, Values and Institutional Structures Which Support Racism, Sexism and Elitism* (Berkeley, Cal: Two Riders Press, 1975) (with co-authors Donald K. Struckmann and Lynn Dorland Trost); "Equality: Beyond Dualism and Oppression," Chapter 6 of *Anatomy of Racism*, ed. David Theo Goldberg (Minneapolis: Univ. of Minnesota Press, 1990); and *How We Are*

Our Enemy—And How to Stop: Our Unfinished Task of Fulfilling the Values of Democracy (Jamaica Plain, Mass.: John L. Hodge, Publisher, 2011).

CHAPTER 4

[22] Although there are no clear lines, I will use "indigenous Americans" and "indigenous peoples" without quotation marks, since these terms refer to a locality and are not in general use as designating a "race." I will put the terms "Native American" and "Indian" in quotation marks, because in general use they are often considered as designating a "race." I sometimes use the terms "Indian" or "Native American" (both in quotation marks), especially "Indian," because it is a short word, to refer to the indigenous peoples of America.

[23] Philip D. Curtin, *Cross-Cultural Trade in World History* (Cambridge, UK: Cambridge Univ. Press, 1984), pp. 84, 179-182, 214-216; Julie Winch, *Between Slavery and Freedom*.

[24] See, for example, John Henry Merryman, *The Civil Law Tradition: An Introduction to the Legal Systems of Western Europe and Latin America*, 2nd ed. (Stanford: Stanford Univ. Press, 1985), Chapter 1, pp. 1 ff.

[25] *The Economist*, "The power of words," Oct. 17, 2015, p. 90.

[26] John M. Barry, *Roger Williams and the Creation of the American Soul* (New York: Viking, 2012), pp. 20-21; *The Economist*, "Magna Carta at 800: The uses of history," Dec. 20, 2014, pp. 34 ff.

[27] Ibid.

[28] Betty Wood, *The Origins of American Slavery* (New York: Hill and Wang, 1997), p. 26; Nigel File and Chris Power, *Black Settlers in Britain 1555-1958* (Oxford: Heinemann International, 1981), p. 5.

[29] Hugh Murray, *Historical Account of Discoveries and Travels in Africa: From the Earliest Ages to the Present Time*, 2nd ed., Vol. 1 (Edinburgh: Printed for Archibald Constable and Co., 1818), pp. 149-150.

[30] Wood, *The Origins of American Slavery*, p. 22.

[31] Barry, *Roger Williams*, pp. 178, 277-278, 340, 356-358.

[32] Ibid., pp. 340, 357-358.

[33] Wood, *The Origins of American Slavery*, pp. 26-27; Jordan, *White Over Black*, p. 59; File & Power, *Black Settlers in Britain*, p. 5.

[34] Ibid.

[35] Wood, *The Origins of American Slavery*, p. 27.

[36] J. Jean Hecht, *Continental and Colonial Servants in Eighteenth Century England*, *Smith College Studies in History*, Vol. XI, Department of History of Smith College, Northampton, Mass., 1954, pp. 33-35.

[37] *Somerset v. Stewart* (1772), 98 ER 499; 12 Geo. 3.

[38] Wood, *The Origins of American Slavery*, pp. 27-28; David Brion Davis, *The Problem of Slavery in Western Culture* (Ithaca, New York: Cornell Univ. Press, 1969), pp. 208-210; Hecht, *Continental and Colonial Servants*, pp. 37-40.

[39] Wood, *The Origins of American Slavery*, p. 28.

[40] File & Power, *Black Settlers in Britain*, p. 1; Hecht, *Continental and Colonial Servants*, p. 34.

[41] File & Power, *Black Settlers in Britain*, pp. 9-14; Hecht, *Continental and Colonial Servants*, pp. 33-40.

[42] File & Power, *Black Settlers in Britain*, p. 2; James Boswell, *The Life of Samuel Johnson* (New York: Alfred A. Knopf, 1992), pp. 146, 146n.2, 354, 1222-1223, 1223n.1.

[43] Jordan, *White Over Black*, p. 15.

[44] Hecht, *Continental and Colonial Servants*, pp.36, 40-50, 56.

[45] See generally: Fredrickson, *Racism: A Short History*; File & Power, *Black Settlers in Britain*.

[46] Jordan, *White Over Black*, pp. 56-57; Wood, *The Origins of American Slavery*, p. 9; D. Davis, *The Problem of Slavery in Western Culture*, p. 8.

[47] Wood, *The Origins of American Slavery*, pp. 37-38; Barry, *Roger Williams*, p. 92.

[48] Wood, *The Origins of American Slavery*, p. 40.

[49] Barry, *Roger Williams*, pp. 92-95.

[50] Jordan, *White Over Black*, p. 44.

[51] Ibid., 89 ff.

[52] Ibid., p. 44; Wood, *The Origins of American Slavery*, p. 40.

[53] Wood, *The Origins of American Slavery*, pp. 22, 28.

[54] Washington Irving, *The Complete Works of Washington Irving*, Part II (Paris: Baudry's European Library, 1834), p. 949.

[55] Jordan, *White Over Black*, p. 44.

[56] Ibid.

[57] Ibid.

[58] Ibid., pp. 74, 122 ff; Johnston Greene, *The Negro in Colonial New England, 1620-1776* (New York: Columbia Univ. Press, 1942), pp. 196 ff, 290 ff; Winch, *Between Slavery and Freedom*, p. 6.

[59] Jordan, *White Over Black,* pp. 95ff, 136 ff.; Winch, *Between Slavery and Freedom*, pp. xiii ff.

[60] Ibid.; and following text.

[61] *Proceeding and Acts of the General Assembly of Maryland* (September, 1664); Jordan, *White Over Black,* p. 79; J. Jones, *A Dreadful Deceit*, p. 43. Winch, *Between Slavery and Freedom*, pp. 7-8.

[62] Jordan, *White Over Black,* p. 79.

[63] Ibid.

[64] Ibid., p. 80.

[65] Pascoe, *What Comes Naturally,* p. 20.

[66] Greene, *The Negro in Colonial New England,* pp. 202 ff.

[67] Ibid., p. 204.

[68] Ibid., p. 207. See Jordan, *White Over Black,* pp. 137 ff.

[69] As a result, it became difficult to determine visually who was supposedly "white" and who "black." See, for example: Pascoe, *What Comes Naturally,* pp. 112 ff.

[70] Greene, *The Negro in Colonial New England,* pp. 208-09.

[71] Ibid., pp. 204-205; Pascoe, *What Comes Naturally*, pp. 24-25.

[72] Greene, *The Negro in Colonial New England,* p. 209.

[73] Ibid., pp. 198 ff.

[74] Ibid., p. 208.

[75] Ibid., pp. 222-24.

[76] Ibid., pp. 201 ff.; Jordan, *White Over Black,* p. 138. See generally: Daniel J. Sharfstein, *The Invisible Line: A Secret History of Race in America* (New York: Penguin Group, 2011), pp. 322-23.

[77] Jordan, *White Over Black,* pp. 136 ff.; Greene, *The Negro in Colonial New England,* pp. 203-204.

[78] See Jordan, *White Over Black,* pp.136 ff.; Greene, *The Negro in Colonial New England,* pp. 206-207.

[79] Greene, *The Negro in Colonial New England,* p. 206.

[80] Jordan, *White Over Black,* p. 139.

[81] Ibid., p. 145.

[82] J. Jones, *A Dreadful Deceit*, p. 52.

[83] Winch, *Between Slavery and Freedom*, p. 70.

[84] Ibid.

[85] Jordan, *White Over Black,* p. 168.

[86] Greene, *The Negro in Colonial New England,* p. 150.

[87] Ibid., pp. 207-08.

[88] Ibid., pp. 198 ff.

142

[89] Jordan, *White Over Black,* pp. 168-69.

[90] Ibid., pp. 169-70.

[91] Ibid., p. 168; see Pascoe, *What Comes Naturally,* pp. 113-114.

[92] Jordan, *White Over Black,* pp. 171-73; Sharfstein, *The Invisible Line,* especially pp. 322-23.

[93] Jordan, *White Over Black,* p. 173.

[94] Ibid., pp. 173-74.

[95] Sharfstein, *The Invisible Line,* pp. 3, 322.

[96] Ibid., p. 322.

[97] W. E. B. DuBois, *The Autobiography of W. E. B. DuBois* (New York: International Publishers, 1968), pp. 137-138.

[98] Madison Hemings, "Life among the Lowly, No. 1," *Pike County Republican,* Pike County, Ohio, March 13, 1873.

[99] Ibid.

[100] Ibid.

[101] Ibid.

[102] (New York: W. W. Norton, 2008).

[103] Frederick Douglass, *Narrative of the Life of Frederick Douglass, An American Slave* (Garden City, New York: Doubleday, 1963), p. 4.

[104] Ibid.

[105] Barry, *Roger Williams,* pp. 5, 214.

[106] Ibid., pp. 308-310.

[107] Ibid., pp. 352-53.

[108] Ibid., p. 356.

[109] See "Rhode island Church Taking Unusual Step to Illuminate Its Slavery Role," *The New York Times,* Aug. 24, 2015, p. A9.

[110] Barry, *Roger Williams,* pp. 181-82, 227, 286-87.

[111] Ibid., pp. 1, 158 - 60.

[112] Ibid., pp. 215-217, 234-35.

[113] Ibid., pp. 133-35.

[114] A history of discrimination against reservation "Indians" in South Dakota including effective denial of their right to vote up to 2004 is described in *Shirt v. Hazeltine,* U.S. District Court, District of South Dakota, 336 F. Supp. 2d 976 (D.S.D. 2004), 1018 - 1034; Laughlin McDonald, "The Voting Rights Act in Indian Country: South Dakota, A Case Study," 29 *American Indian Law Review* 43 (2004–2005). The Voting Rights Act of 1965 was not extended to "Indians" until 1975. Pub. L. No. 94-73, §§ 203, 204, 89 Stat. 400, 401–03 (1975) (codified as amended at 42 U.S.C. §§ 1973a to 1973c (2000)): McDonald, "The Voting Rights Act in Indian Country," p. 43.

[115] Robert S. Tilton, *Pocahontas: The Evolution of an American Narrative* (New York: Cambridge Univ. Press, 1994), pp. 9-11.

[116] See following text.

[117] Tilton, *Pocahontas*, p. 31.

[118] Oswalt, *This Land Was Theirs*, p. 517.

[119] Greene, *The Negro in Colonial New England*, pp. 198-200.

[120] Helen C. Roundtree, *Pocahontas's People: The Powhatan "Indians" of Virginia Through Four Centuries* (Norman: Univ. of Oklahoma Press, 1989), pp. 178-79.

[121] Ibid., p. 180.

[122] Ibid., pp. 180-190.

[123] Winch, *Between Slavery and Freedom*, pp. 8-9.

[124] Ibid., p. 10.

[125] Byran Sykes, *DNA USA: A Genetic Portrait of America* (New York: Liveright Pub., 2012), p. 282.

[126] Lynwood Montell, "The Coe Ridge Colony: A Racial Island Disappears," *American Anthropologist*, Vol. 74, Issue 3, pp. 710 ff. (1972); William Lynwood Montell, *The Saga of Coe Ridge* (Knoxville: Univ. of Tennessee Press, 1970). William S. Pollitzer, "The Physical Anthropology and Genetics of Marginal People of the Southeastern United States," *American Anthropologist*, Vol. 74, Issue 3, pp. 719, 723 (1972).

[127] Pollitzer, "The Physical Anthropology and Genetics of Marginal People of the Southeastern United States," pp. 719 ff.

[128] Andrew R. Graybill, *The Red and the White* (New York: Liveright Publishing, 2013).

[129] Ibid., p. 48.

[130] Ibid., p. 50.

[131] Sykes, *DNA USA*, pp. 259-262.

[132] *Encyclopedia of World Biography*, 2nd ed., Vol. 21 (Detroit: Gale, 2004), pp. 99-100.

[133] Sykes, *DNA USA*, pp. 46-49.

CHAPTER 5

[134] Claudius Ptolemy, *The Geography*, trans. and edited by Edward Luther Stevenson (New York: Dover Publications, 1991).

[135] Jerry H. Bentley, *Old World Encounters: Cross-Cultural Contacts and Exchanges in Pre-Modern Times* (New York: Oxford Univ. Press, 1993), p. 20.

[136] See generally Bentley, *Old World Encounters*;; Curtin, *Cross-Cultural Trade*.

[137] Bentley, *Old World Encounters*, p. vii.

[138] Curtin, *Cross-Cultural Trade*, pp. 64-65, 71.

[139] Bentley, *Old World Encounters*, pp. 20-21.

[140] Curtin, *Cross-Cultural Trade*, pp. 64-65, 71-77; Martin Meredith, *The Fortunes of Africa: A 5000-Year History of Wealth, Greed, and Endeavor* (New York: Public Affairs, 2014), pp. 24-29.

[141] Curtin, *Cross-Cultural Trade*, pp. 77-78.

[142] Lindsay Allen, *The Persian Empire* (Chicago: Univ. of Chicago Press, 2005), pp. 133 ff.

[143] Bentley, *Old World Encounters*, p. 46.

[144] Ibid., pp. 46-47, 53-54; Paul K. Davis, *Encyclopedia of Invasions and Conquests from Ancient Times to the Present* (Santa Barbara: ABC-CLIO, 1996), pp. 24-25, 46.

[145] Valerie Hansen, *The Silk Road: A New History* (New York: Oxford Univ. Press, 2012), p. 30.

[146] P. Davis, *Encyclopedia of Invasions and Conquests*, pp. 24-25.

[147] See L. Allen, *The Persian Empire*.

[148] P. Davis, *Encyclopedia of Invasions and Conquests*, p. 25; see L. Allen, *The Persian Empire* , p. 150.

[149] L. Allen, *The Persian Empire,* p. 136.

[150] Ibid., p. 147.

[151] Graybill, *The Red and the White*, p. 48.

[152] Ibid., pp. 49-50.

[153] Roundtree, *Pocahontas's People,* pp. 59-61.

[154] Meredith, *The Fortunes of Africa*, pp. 5-6.

[155] Richard A. Gabriel, *Hannibal: The Military Biography of Rome's Greatest Enemy* (Washington, D.C.: Potomac Books, 2011), pp. 86, 87.

[156] Ibid., pp. xi, 57 ff.

[157] P. Davis, *Encyclopedia of Invasions and Conquests*, pp. 31-33; Peter Heather, *The Fall of the Roman Empire: A New History of Rome and the Barbarians* (New York: Oxford Univ. Press, 2006), p. 273.

[158] Bentley, *Old World Encounters*, p. 23.

[159] Matt Waters, *Ancient Persia: A Concise History of the Achaemenid Empire, 550–330 BCE* (New York: Cambridge Univ. Press, 2014), pp. 5-7.

[160] Heather, *The Fall of the Roman Empire*, p. 263.

[161] D. Davis, *The Problem of Slavery in Western Culture*, pp. 32 ff, 62-90.

[162] Derek Williams, *Romans and Barbarians* (New York: St. Martin's Press, 1999), p. 3; Derek Williams, *Romans and Barbarians: Four Views from the Empire's Edge, 1ˢᵗ Century A.D.* (New York: St. Martin's Press, 1998), pp. 3-4.

[163] *The Economist,* "Nothing idyllic," January 11, 2014, p. 42.

[164] Jaroslav R. Vávra, *5000 Years of Glass-Making: The History of Glass,* trans. I. R. Gottheiner (Prague: Artia, 1954), pp. 15 ff.

[165] *The Economist,* "Dirty sheets and stray cats," June 20, 2015, p. 48.

[166] Uta C. Merzbach and Carl B. Boyer, *History of Mathematics,* 3ʳᵈ ed. (Hoboken, New Jersey: John Wiley & Sons, 2011), chs. 2, 3, 4, 9 & 10.

[167] Ibid., p. 189.

[168] Hansen, *The Silk Road,* p. 15.

[169] Malcolm Todd, *The Everyday Life of The Barbarians: Goths, Franks and Vandals* (New York: G. P. Putnam's Sons, 1972), pp. 72-87, 107-108, 158-159, 163, 169.

[170] Chris Scarre, *Chronicle of the Roman Emperors* (London: Thames & Hudson, 1995), pp. 60-64; 126-130; 160-164; 229-232.

[171] Heather, *The Fall of the Roman Empire,* p. 467.

[172] See, for example, Gabriel, *Hannibal,* pp. 1-3, 17-18, 60, 63; Allen, *The Persian Empire,* pp. 133 ff.; Christopher Kelly, *The Roman Empire: A Very Short Introduction* (Oxford: Oxford Univ. Press, 2006), pp. 14-22, 82-84.

[173] Kelly, *The Roman Empire,* pp. 14-22.

[174] Ibid., p. 14.

[175] See, for example, Todd, *The Everyday Life of The Barbarians;* Derek Williams, *Romans and Barbarians.*

[176] Chris Scarre, *The Penguin Historical Atlas of Ancient Rome* (London: Penguin Books, 1995), pp. 24-25, 30.

[177] Ibid., pp. 75, 80-81, 86-87, 96-97; Kelly, *The Roman Empire,* p. 1.

[178] Gabriel, *Hannibal,* pp. 61 ff.; P. Davis, *Encyclopedia of Invasions and Conquests,* p. 59; Scarre, *The Penguin Historical Atlas of Ancient Rome,* pp. 24-25; Kelly, *The Roman Empire,* pp. 5-6.

[179] Gabriel, *Hannibal,* pp. 61 ff.

[180] Ibid., especially pp. 21 ff., 70 ff., 85-87, 101 ff.; Leonard Cottrell, *Hannibal: Enemy of Rome* (Boston: Da Capo Press, 1992), p. 26; Scarre, *The Penguin Historical Atlas of Ancient Rome,* pp. 24-25; Kelly, *The Roman Empire,* pp. 5-6.

[181] Gabriel, *Hannibal,* p. 14.

[182] Gabriel, *Hannibal,* p. 73; P. Davis, *Encyclopedia of Invasions and Conquests,* p. 44.

146

[183] Scarre, *The Penguin Historical Atlas of Ancient Rome*, pp. 26-27, 63, 74-75.

[184] Sykes, *DNA USA*, pp. 129-130.

[185] Scarre, *The Penguin Historical Atlas of Ancient Rome*, pp. 80-81; Heather, *The Fall of the Roman Empire*, p. 273.

[186] Scarre, *The Penguin Historical Atlas of Ancient Rome*, pp. 80-81.

[187] Curtin, *Cross-Cultural Trade*, pp. 99-100.

[188] Ibid., p. 100.

[189] See Kelly, *The Roman Empire*, p. 6; Scarre, *The Penguin Historical Atlas of Ancient Rome*, pp. 41-42.

[190] Scarre, *Chronicle of the Emperors*, pp. 130, 131, 133, 138, 146, 148-152, 153, 166-167, 171.

[191] For example, see Michael Brett and Elizabeth Fentress, *The Berbers* (Oxford: Blackwell Publishing, 1996), pp. 50-53; Heather, *The Fall of the Roman Empire*, pp. 434-435.

[192] Peter Heather, *The Fall of the Roman Empire*, pp. 474.

[193] Ibid., p. 475.

[194] Ibid., p. 473.

[195] Ibid., p. 394.

[196] See Scarre, *Chronicle of the Emperors*, pp. 159-232; Scarre, *The Penguin Historical Atlas of Ancient Rome*, pp. 132-133. See generally, Heather, *The Fall of the Roman Empire*.

[197] Heather, *The Fall of the Roman Empire*, pp. 146, 151-154, 204-205, 433-435, 450 ff.; Scarre, *The Penguin Historical Atlas of Ancient Rome*, p. 132.

[198] Heather, *The Fall of the Roman Empire*, pp. 145-146.

[199] Scarre, *The Penguin Historical Atlas of Ancient Rome*, pp. 132-133.

[200] Heather, *The Fall of the Roman Empire*, p. 191.

[201] Ibid., pp. 197-198; 263-270, 461; Scarre, *The Penguin Historical Atlas of Ancient Rome*, pp. 132-133.

[202] Heather, *The Fall of the Roman Empire*, pp. 146-151, 450.

[203] Ibid., pp. 151, 319; Todd, *The Everyday Life of The Barbarians*, p. 13.

[204] Heather, *The Fall of the Roman Empire*, pp. 153-156.

[205] Ibid., p. 153.

[206] Ibid., p. 300.

[207] Ibid., pp. 300-342.

[208] Ibid., p. 329.

[209] Ibid., pp. 313-342, 360-365; Peter Heather, *Empires and Barbarians: The Fall of Rome and the Birth of Europe* (New York: Oxford Univ. Press, 2010), pp. 207-221, 238-265.

[210] Heather, *The Fall of the Roman Empire*, p. 342.

[211] Ibid., pp. 351-384.

[212] Ibid., p. 486; Scarre, *Chronicle of the Emperors*, p. 232.

[213] Heather, *The Fall of the Roman Empire*, pp. 435, 450 ff.; Heather, *Empires and Barbarians*, pp. 383-384; Scarre, *The Penguin Historical Atlas of Ancient Rome*, p. 132.

[214] Heather, *Empires and Barbarians*, pp. 333 ff.

[215] Heather, *The Fall of the Roman Empire*, p. 317.

[216] For example, *The Economist* noted the "mass rapes of German women by the Allies" during World War II. "Guilt and reconciliation," May 2, 2015, p. 44.

[217] Heather, *The Fall of the Roman Empire*, pp. 371, 466.

[218] Ibid., pp. 390, 373-374, 376.

[219] Ibid., pp. 393, 462.

[220] Ibid., p. 463.

[221] Ibid., pp. 321, 335-336, 469.

[222] Virgie Hoban, "Researchers suggest another ancestry for Native Americans," *The Boston Globe*, July 22, 2015, p. A1.

[223] Curtin, *Cross-Cultural Trade*, p. 11; Bentley, *Old World Encounters*, pp. 33-35; Hansen, *The Silk Road,* p. 235.

[224] Bentley, *Old World Encounters*, pp. 26, 32-34; Hansen, *The Silk Road*, pp. 235-236; Curtin, *Cross-Cultural Trade*, p. 93; see generally, Hansen, *The Silk Road*.

[225] Bentley, *Old World Encounters*, p. 32.

[226] Hansen, *The Silk Road,* p. 238.

[227] Ibid., pp. 238-241; Bentley, *Old World Encounters*, pp. 67 ff.

[228] Hansen, *The Silk Road*.

[229] Ibid., p. 13.

[230] Ibid., pp. 13-14.

[231] Ibid., p. 26.

[232] Ibid., pp. 30-31.

[233] Ibid., pp. 21, 66.

[234] Ibid., pp. 68-69.

[235] Ibid., pp. 83 ff.

[236] Bentley, *Old World Encounters*, pp. 36-41.

[237] Ibid.

[238] See discussion of these influences in Hodge, et al., *Cultural Bases of Racism and Group Oppression*, especially Part IV. See also Wayland Young, *Eros Denied* (New York: Grove Press, 1964).

[239] *The Complete Works of Washington Irving*, Part II.

[240] Ibid.; Meredith, *The Fortunes of Africa*, pp. 65-67; Jo Ann H. Moran Cruz and Richard Gerberding, *Medieval Worlds: An Introduction to European History, 300-1492* (Boston: Houghton Mifflin, 2004), pp. 204 ff., 424; Marion Kaplan, *The Portuguese: The Land and its People* (Manchester, U.K.: Carcanet Press, 2006), p. 5.

[241] Kaplan, *The Portuguese*, p. 6.

[242] Cruz, *Medieval Worlds*, pp. 206-207; *The Economist*, "The mosque in the cathedral," Oct. 10, 2015, p. 54; Kaplan, *The Portuguese*, pp. 9-10.

[243] *Andalusia* (Firenze, Italy: Bonechi, 2002) (collaborative work); *The Economist*, "The mosque in the cathedral," Oct. 10, 2015, p. 54 Kaplan, *The Portuguese*, pp. 6 ff.

[244] Kaplan, *The Portuguese*, pp. 6 ff.

[245] Ibid., pp. 28 ff.; Curtin, *Cross-Cultural Trade*, pp. 136 ff.

[246] Kaplan, *The Portuguese*, pp. 30-31 (map), 28 ff; Curtin, *Cross-Cultural Trade*, pp. 34-35, 136 ff.

[247] Meredith, *The Fortunes of Africa*, pp. 107-110, 170-171.

[248] Curtin, *Cross-Cultural Trade*,, p. 180.

[249] Meredith, *The Fortunes of Africa*, pp. 65-67.

[250] Ibid., p. 65.

[251] Ibid., pp. 81-83.

[252] Ibid, p. 78-79, 81-83.

[253] Ibid, p. 78.

[254] Cruz, *Medieval Worlds*, pp. 185, 194.

[255] Frank McLynn, *Genghis Khan: His Conquests, His Empire, His Legacy* (Boston: Da Capo Press, 2015), p. 330.

[256] Cruz, *Medieval Worlds*, pp. 194-195.

[257] Ibid, p. 194.

[258] Ibid., pp.. 185 ff.

[259] Ibid., pp. 186, 190, 428.

[260] McLynn, *Genghis Kahn*, pp. xxix ff., xxxvi, 217, 330, 410, 432, 438 ff., 458 ff., 476, 478, 488, 489. The quotation is from page 489. Cruz, *Medieval Worlds*, pp. 428 ff.

[261] McLynn, *Genghis Kahn*, pp. 496-497, 506 ff.

[262] Ibid., pp. 412 ff.

[263] Ibid., pp. 159-160, 414.

[264] Ibid., 171-174, 323, 486-487, 502; Jack Weatherford, *The Secret History of the Mongol Queens: How the Daughters of Genghis Khan Rescued His Empire* (New York: Crown Publishers, 2010).

[265] McLynn, *Genghis Kahn*, p., 172.

[266] Ibid., pp. 111 ff.

[267] Hansen, *The Silk Road*, p. 229.

[268] McLynn, *Genghis Kahn*, pp. 262, 264, 330, 370, 503.

[269] Ibid., pp. 502-503.

[270] Ibid., pp. 276, 280, 383, 457, 466, 475-476.

[271] Ibid., 139-140, 144, 145, 151, 168-171.

[272] Ibid., 139-140, 144, 145, 151, 163-165, 168-171, 564.

[273] Ibid., p. 491.

[274] Ibid., pp. 490-491.

[275] Ibid., pp. 54, 477, 484, 486.

CHAPTER 6

[276] Jacques Barzun, *Race: A Study in Superstition* (New York: Harper & Row, 1965; originally published in 1937); Ashley Montagu, *Man's Most Dangerous Myth: The Fallacy of Race*, 4th ed. (Cleveland: World Pub. Co., 1964; 1st ed. originally published in 1942); W. E. B. Du Bois, *Dusk of Dawn* (New York: Schocken Books, 1968; originally published in 1940), ch. 5 and see ch. 6. See also *The Concept of Race*, ed. Ashley Montagu (London: Collier Books, 1969).

[277] *The Descent of Man*, pp. 194 ff.

[278] See, for example, the references in the preceding two notes.

[279] *The Economist*, "Breaking the code," Aug. 8, 2015, p. 71.

[280] Montagu, *The Concept of Race*, ch. I, p. 7. This chapter was originally presented as a lecture in April, 1941, before the American Association of Physical Anthropologists, and originally published in 1941, titled "The Meaninglessness of the Anthropological Conception of Race," in *The Journal of Heredity*, Vol. 23, 1941, pp. 243-247. Ibid., p. 1 (note).

[281] Ibid., p. 7.

[282] Theodosius Dobzhansky, *Genetics and the Origin of Species* (New York: Columbia Univ. Press, 1st ed., 1937). See Montagu, *Man's Most Dangerous Myth*, pp. 76-77, 80; Michael Yudell, II, "A Short History of the Race Concept," in *Race and the Genetic Revolution: Science, Myth, and Culture*, ed. Sheldon Krimsky and Kathleen Sloan (New York: Columbia Univ. Press, 2011), pp. 20-21.

[283] Montagu, *The Concept of Race*, ch. I.

[284] (Lanham, Maryland: AltaMira Press).

[285] Montagu, *Man's Most Dangerous Myth*, p. 76.

[286] Sheldon Krimsky and Kathleen Sloan, ed., *Race and the Genetic Revolution: Science, Myth, and Culture* (New York: Columbia Univ. Press, 2011).

[287] Sykes, *DNA USA*, p. 275.

[288] See generally Barzun, *Race: A Study in Superstition;* Montagu, *Man's Most Dangerous Myth;* Du Bois, *Dusk of Dawn*, chs. 5 and 6; Montagu, *The Concept of Race;* Krimsky and Sloan, *Race and the Genetic Revolution.*

[289] Jacobus tenBroek, et al., *Prejudice, War and the Constitution* (Berkeley: Univ. of California Press, 1970); Alexis Marie Adams, "Site recalls WWII fear, injustice," *Boston Sunday Globe*, June 7, 2015, M6.

[290] See "Voting Rights in Indian Country: A Special Report of the Voting Rights Project of the American Civil Liberties Union," ACLU, 2009.

[291] Svante Pääbo, *Neanderthal Man: In Search of Lost Genomes* (New York: Basic Books, 2014).

[292] Ruth Graham, "Almost Human," *Boston Globe*, February 15, 2015, p. K1, K4. See *The Economist*, "Probing the chamber of secrets," June 21, 2014, p. 75; and *The Economist*, "Ecce Homo naledi," Sept. 12, 2015, p. 76.

[293] Pääbo, *Neanderthal Man*, pp. 185-200, 237.

[294] Ibid., p. 208.

[295] Ibid., pp. 197 ff., 208.

[296] Ibid., p. 237.

[297] Ibid.

[298] *The Economist*, "Greater than the sum of its parts," Oct. 31, 2015, p. 75. The article reports on a new animal that is a mixture of coyote, wolf and dog, and has acquired the strengths of all three.

[299] Pääbo, *Neanderthal Man*, pp. 237-253.

[300] Darwin recorded many new mixtures in *The Descent of Man*, Chapter 7, pp. 202 ff.

[301] Du Bois, *Dusk of Dawn*, p. 109.

[302] Ibid., p. 103.

[303] Sykes, *DNA USA*, pp. 229, 312.

[304] Ibid., p. 312.

[305] Ibid., pp. 238, 239.

[306] Ibid., pp. 245-247, 312.

[307] Ibid., p. 231.

[308] Ibid., pp. 282-284.

[309] Ibid., p. 289.

[310] Ibid., p. 311.

[311] Ibid., pp. 310-311.

[312] Ibid., p. 310.

[313] Ibid., p. 311.

[314] Ibid., pp. 313-314.

[315] Ibid., p. 313.

[316] Montagu, *Man's Most Dangerous Myth*, p. 76; see generally Krimsky and Sloan, *Race and the Genetic Revolution*.

[317] Robert J. Sternberg, et al., "Intelligence, Race, and Genetics," in *Race and the Genetic Revolution*, Krimsky and Sloan, p. 206.

CHAPTER 7

[318] As Jean-Paul Sartre stated about anti-Semitism, "The anti-Semite is impervious to reason and to experience." *Anti-Semite and Jew*, trans. George J. Becker (New York: Schocken Books, 1948), p. 20.

[319] See Sheryll Cashin, *Place not Race: A New Vision of Opportunity in America* (Boston: Beacon Press, 2014), p. 31; *The Economist*, "From the hood to Harvard," May 2, 2015, p. 26.

CHAPTER 8

[320] Alfred North Whitehead, *Science and the Modern World* (New York: Mentor Books, 1959); originally published in 1925.

[321] Ibid., p. 52.

[322] Ibid., p. 55.

[323] *The Economist*, "Science's great leap forward," July 7, 2012, p. 13.

[324] "For starters, let's agree that there is no 'white America' or 'black America,'" *Boston Sunday Globe*, Aug. 24, 2014, K12.

[325] Ta-Nehisi Coates, *Between the World and Me* (New York: Spiegel & Grau, 2015).

Although Coates asserts that his views are personal and should not be viewed as reflecting "the black experience," he nonetheless conveys this construct to his son and his readers. Renée Graham, "The world of Ta-Nehisi Coates," *Boston Globe*, Oct. 20, 2015, p. A8.

[326] See Ralph Young, *Dissent: The History of an American Idea* (New York: New York Univ. Press, 2015).

[327] The assumption is apparent in the paragraph spanning pages 78-79.

[328] I explained the distorting influence of wealth on electoral politics, and what should be done about it, in "Democracy and Free Speech: A Normative Theory of Society and Government," Chapter 5 of *The First Amendment Reconsidered*, ed. Bill F. Chamberlin and Charlene J. Brown (New York: Longman, 1982), pp. 148 ff.

[329] An excellent probe into unconscious racism is Debbie Irving's *Waking Up White and Finding Myself in the Story of Race* (Cambridge, Mass: Elephant Room Press, 2014).

CHAPTER 9

[330] Terry Anderson, *The Pursuit of Fairness: A History of Affirmative Action* (New York: Oxford Univ. Press, 2004), esp. Chapter 2.

[331] Mary L. Dudziak, *Cold War Civil Rights: Race and the Image of American Democracy* (Princeton, New Jersey: Princeton Univ. Press, paperback reissue 2011), p. 6.

[332] Anderson, *The Pursuit of Fairness*, p. 99.

[333] Ibid., pp. 100 ff.

[334] See notes above for Chapter 7.

[335] Cashin, *Place not Race*, p. 74.

[336] Ibid., pp. 110-111.

[337] Rhona S. Weinstein, *Reaching Higher: The Power of Expectations in Schooling* (Cambridge, Mass.: Harvard Univ. Press, 2002), p. 1.

[338] See generally ibid. See also the paper described in *The Economist*, "University challenge," January 17, 2015, pp. 74 – 75, which suggests that "it could . . . be that women and black people themselves, through exposure to a culture that constantly tells them (which research suggests it does) that they do not have an aptitude for things like maths and physics, have come to believe this is true." p. 75.

[339] Cashin, *Place not Race*, p. 74.

[340] "On your toes," *The Economist*, April 18, 2015, p. 78, discussing *Work Rules! Insight from Inside Google that Will Transform How You Live and Lead*, by Laszlo Bock.

[341] Weinstein, *Reaching Higher*, p. 302.

[342] Peter Schworm, "SAT losing favor as more colleges end requirement," *The Boston Globe*, Nov. 6, 2015, p. A1.

[343] The conflict between the values of democracy and those of elitism are explained in three of my previous writings listed in note 21 (chapter 3) above.

CHAPTER 10

[344] Hodge, *Cultural Bases of Racism and Group Oppression*, p. 2.

[345] This phenomenon was noted in *The Economist*, "American Baptists: Dipped in controversy," p. 80, June 13, 2015. This article is a review of *Baptists in America: A History*, by Thomas Kidd and Barry Hankins (Oxford Univ. Press, 2015).

[346] Michael Dennis, *Luther P. Jackson and a Life for Civil Rights* (Gainesville: Univ. Press of Florida, 2004).

CHAPTER 11

[347] I discuss the values of democracy in *How We Are Our Enemy—And How to Stop: Our Unfinished Task of Fulfilling the Values of Democracy.*

[348] I discuss how to remedy some of these issues in Chapter 5 of *How We Are Our Enemy—And How to Stop.* A manifestation of this class structure is the underfunding of schools in poorer communities: see, for example, *The Boston Sunday Globe*, "Old battle lines drawn anew in Kansas," by Michael Kranish, April 26. 2015, p. A1.

[349] See *How We Are our Enemy—And How to Stop.*

BIBLIOGRAPHY

Books, Book Chapters and Journals

Allen, Lindsay, *The Persian Empire* (Chicago: Univ. of Chicago Press, 2005).

Anderson, Terry H., *The Pursuit of Fairness: A History of Affirmative Action* (New York: Oxford Univ. Press, 2004).

Anderson, Terry, *The Pursuit of Fairness: A History of Affirmative Action* (New York: Oxford Univ. Press, 2004).

Barry, John M., *Roger Williams and the Creation of the American Soul* (New York: Viking, 2012).

Barzun, Jacques, *Race: A Study in Superstition* (New York: Harper & Row, 1965; originally published in 1937).

Bentley, Jerry H., *Old World Encounters: Cross-Cultural Contacts and Exchanges in Pre-Modern Times* (New York: Oxford Univ. Press, 1993).

Boswell, James, *The Life of Samuel Johnson* (New York: Alfred A. Knopf, 1992).

Brett, Michael and Elizabeth Fentress, *The Berbers* (Oxford: Blackwell Publishing, 1996).

Buster, Greene B., *Brighter Sun* (New York: Pageant Press, 1954).

Cashin, Sheryll, *Place not Race: A New Vision of Opportunity in America* (Boston: Beacon Press, 2014).

Coates, Ta-Nehisi, *Between the World and Me* (New York: Spiegel & Grau, 2015).

Cottrell, Leonard, *Hannibal: Enemy of Rome* (Boston: Da Capo Press, 1992).

Cruz, Jo Ann H. Moran and Richard Gerberding, *Medieval Worlds: An Introduction to European History, 300-1492* (Boston: Houghton Mifflin, 2004).

Curtin, Philip D., *Cross-Cultural Trade in World History* (Cambridge, UK: Cambridge Univ. Press, 1984).

Darwin, Charles, *The Descent of Man* (London: Penguin Books, 2004).

Davis, David Brion, *The Problem of Slavery in Western Culture* (Ithaca, New York: Cornell Univ. Press, 1969).

Davis, Paul K., *Encyclopedia of Invasions and Conquests from Ancient Times to the Present* (Santa Barbara: ABC-CLIO, 1996).

de Beauvoir, Simone, *The Second Sex*, H. M. Parshley, trans & ed. (New York: Bantam Books, 1961; originally published in French in 1949).

Dennis, Michael, *Luther P. Jackson and a Life for Civil Rights* (Gainesville: Univ. Press of Florida, 2004).

Dobzhansky, Theodosius, *Genetics and the Origin of Species* (New York: Columbia Univ. Press, 1st ed., 1937).

Douglass, Frederick, *Narrative of the Life of Frederick Douglass, An American Slave* (Garden City, New York: Doubleday, 1963).

Du Bois, W. E. B., *Dusk of Dawn* (New York: Schocken Books, 1968; originally published in 1940).

DuBois, W. E. B., *The Autobiography of W. E. B. DuBois* (New York: International Publishers, 1968).

Dudziak, Mary L., *Cold War Civil Rights: Race and the Image of American Democracy* (Princeton, New Jersey: Princeton Univ. Press, paperback reissue 2011).

Encyclopedia of World Biography, 2nd ed., Vol. 21 (Detroit: Gale, 2004).

Estes, Kelli, *The Girl Who Wrote in Silk* (Naperville, Illinois: Sourcebooks, 2015).

File, Nigel and Chris Power, *Black Settlers in Britain 1555-1958* (Oxford: Heinemann International, 1981).

Fredrickson, George M., *The Arrogance of Race: Historical Perspectives on Slavery, Racism, and Social Inequality* (Hanover, New Hampshire: Wesleyan Univ. Press, 1988).

Fredrickson, George M., *Racism: A Short History* (Princeton, New Jersey: Princeton Univ. Press, 2002).

Friedan, Betty, *The Feminine Mystique* (New York: Dell Publishing Co., 1963).

Gabriel, Richard A., *Hannibal: The Military Biography of Rome's Greatest Enemy* (Washington, D.C.: Potomac Books, 2011).

Gordon-Reed, Annette, *The Hemingses of Monticello* (New York: W. W. Norton, 2008).

Graybill, Andrew R., *The Red and the White* (New York: Liveright Publishing, 2013).

Greene, Johnston, *The Negro in Colonial New England, 1620-1776* (New York: Columbia Univ. Press, 1942).

Hansen, Valerie, *The Silk Road: A New History* (New York: Oxford Univ. Press, 2012).

Heather, Peter, *Empires and Barbarians: The Fall of Rome and the Birth of Europe* (New York: Oxford Univ. Press, 2010).

Heather, Peter, *The Fall of the Roman Empire: A New History of Rome and the Barbarians* (New York: Oxford Univ. Press, 2006).

Hecht, J. Jean, *Continental and Colonial Servants in Eighteenth Century England, Smith College Studies in History*, Vol. XI, Department of History of Smith College, Northampton, Mass., 1954.

Hernton, Calvin C., *Sex and Racism in America* (New York: Grove Press, 1965).

Hodge, John L., "Democracy and Free Speech: A Normative Theory of Society and Government," Chapter 5 of *The First Amendment Reconsidered*, ed. Bill F. Chamberlin and Charlene J. Brown (New York: Longman, 1982).

Hodge, John L., "Equality: Beyond Dualism and Oppression," Chapter 6 of *Anatomy of Racism*, ed. David Theo Goldberg (Minneapolis: Univ. of Minnesota Press, 1990).

Hodge, John L, *How We Are Our Enemy—And How to Stop* (Jamaica Plain, Mass.: John L. Hodge, Publisher, 2011).

Hodge, John L., Donald K. Struckmann and Lynn Dorland Trost, *Cultural Bases of Racism and Group Oppression: An Examination of Traditional "Western" Concepts, Values and Institutional Structures Which Support Racism, Sexism and Elitism* (Berkeley, Cal: Two Riders Press, 1975).

Irving, Debbie, *Waking Up White and Finding Myself in the Story of Race* (Cambridge, Mass: Elephant Room Press, 2014).

Irving, Washington *The Complete Works of Washington Irving*, Part II (Paris: Baudry's European Library, 1834).

Jones, Jacqueline, *A Dreadful Deceit: The Myth of Race from the Colonial Era to Obama's America* (New York: Basic Books, 2013).

Jordan, Winthrop, *White Over Black: American Attitudes Toward the Negro, 1550-1812* (Baltimore: Penguin Books, 1969).

Kaplan, Marion, *The Portuguese: The Land and its People* (Manchester, U.K.: Carcanet Press, 2006).

Kelly, Christopher, *The Roman Empire: A Very Short Introduction* (Oxford: Oxford Univ. Press, 2006).

Krimsky, Sheldon and Kathleen Sloan, ed., *Race and the Genetic Revolution: Science, Myth, and Culture* (New York: Columbia Univ. Press, 2011).

McDonald, Laughlin, "The Voting Rights Act in Indian Country: South Dakota, A Case Study," 29 *American Indian Law Review* 43 (2004–2005).

McLynn, Frank, *Genghis Khan: His Conquests, His Empire, His Legacy* (Boston: Da Capo Press, 2015)

Meredith, Martin, *The Fortunes of Africa: A 5000-Year History of Wealth, Greed, and Endeavor* (New York: Public Affairs, 2014).

Merryman, John Henry, *The Civil Law Tradition: An Introduction to the Legal Systems of Western Europe and Latin America*, 2nd ed. (Stanford: Stanford Univ. Press, 1985).

Merzbach, Uta C. and Carl B. Boyer, *History of Mathematics*, 3rd ed. (Hoboken, New Jersey: John Wiley & Sons, 2011).

Montagu, Ashley, "The Meaninglessness of the Anthropological Conception of Race," *The Journal of Heredity*, Vol. 23, 1941, pp. 243-247; originally published in Ashley Montagu, ed., *The Concept of Race*, p. 1.

Montagu, Ashley, ed., *The Concept of Race* (London: Collier Books, 1969).

Montagu, Ashley, *Man's Most Dangerous Myth: The Fallacy of Race*, 4th ed. (Cleveland: World Pub. Co., 1964); 1st ed. originally published in 1942; sixth ed. (Lanham, Maryland: AltaMira Press, 1997).

Montell, Lynwood, "The Coe Ridge Colony: A Racial Island Disappears," *American Anthropologist*, Vol. 74, Issue 3, pp. 710 ff., 1972.

Montell, William Lynwood, *The Saga of Coe Ridge* (Knoxville: Univ. of Tennessee Press, 1970).

Montell, William Lynwood, *The Saga of Coe Ridge* (Knoxville: Univ. of Tennessee Press, 1970).

Morrison, Toni, *A Mercy* (New York: Alfred A. Knopf, 2008).

Murray, Hugh, *Historical Account of Discoveries and Travels in Africa: From the Earliest Ages to the Present Time*, 2nd ed., Vol. 1 (Edinburgh: Printed for Archibald Constable and Co., 1818).

Oswalt, Wendell H., *This Land Was Theirs: A Study of the North American Indian* (New York: John Wiley & Sons, 1966).

Pääbo, Svante, *Neanderthal Man: In Search of Lost Genomes* (New York: Basic Books, 2014).

Pascoe, Peggy, *What Comes Naturally: Miscegenation Law and the Making of Race in America* (New York: Oxford Univ. Press, 2009).

Pollitzer, William S., "The Physical Anthropology and Genetics of Marginal People of the Southeastern United States," *American Anthropologist*, Vol. 74, Issue 3, pp. 719 ff,1972.

Ptolemy, Claudius, *The Geography*, trans. and edited by Edward Luther Stevenson (New York: Dover Publications, 1991).

Roundtree,Helen C., *Pocahontas's People: The Powhatan "Indians" of Virginia Through Four Centuries* (Norman: Univ. of Oklahoma Press, 1989).

Scarre, Chris, *Chronicle of the Roman Emperors* (London: Thames & Hudson, 1995).

Scarre, Chris, *The Penguin Historical Atlas of Ancient Rome* (London: Penguin Books, 1995).

Sharfstein, Daniel J., *The Invisible Line: A Secret History of Race in America* (New York: Penguin Group, 2011).

Silberman, Charles E., *Crisis in Black and White* (New York: Vintage Books, 1964).

Sternberg, Robert J., et al., "Intelligence, Race, and Genetics," *Race and the Genetic Revolution: Science, Myth, and Culture*, ed. Sheldon Krimsky and Kathleen Sloan (New York: Columbia Univ. Press, 2011).

Sykes, Byran, *DNA USA: A Genetic Portrait of America* (New York: Liveright Pub., 2012).

tenBroek, Jacobus, et al., *Prejudice, War and the Constitution* (Berkeley: Univ. of California Press, 1970).

Tilton, Robert S., *Pocahontas: The Evolution of an American Narrative* (New York: Cambridge Univ. Press, 1994).

Todd, Malcolm, *The Everyday Life of The Barbarians: Goths, Franks and Vandals* (New York: G. P. Putnam's Sons, 1972).

Vávra, Jaroslav R., *5000 Years of Glass-Making: The History of Glass,* trans. I. R. Gottheiner (Prague: Artia, 1954).

Waters, Matt, *Ancient Persia: A Concise History of the Achaemenid Empire, 550–330 BCE* (New York: Cambridge Univ. Press, 2014).

Weatherford, Jack, *The Secret History of the Mongol Queens: How the Daughters of Genghis Khan Rescued His Empire* (New York: Crown Publishers, 2010).

Weinstein, Rhona S., *Reaching Higher: The Power of Expectations in Schooling* (Cambridge, Mass.: Harvard Univ. Press, 2002).

Whitehead, Alfred North, *Science and the Modern World* (New York: Mentor Books, 1959; originally published in 1925).

Williams, Derek, *Romans and Barbarians* (New York: St. Martin's Press, 1999).

Williams, Derek, *Romans and Barbarians: Four Views from the Empire's Edge, 1ˢᵗ Century A.D.* (New York: St. Martin's Press, 1998).

Winch, Julie, *Between Slavery and Freedom* (Lanham, Maryland: Rowland & Littlefield, 2014).

Wood, Betty, *The Origins of American Slavery* (New York: Hill and Wang, 1997).

Young, Ralph, *Dissent: The History of an American Idea* (New York: New York Univ. Press, 2015).

Young, Wayland, *Eros Denied* (New York: Grove Press, 1964).

Yudell II, Michael, "A Short History of the Race Concept," *Race and the Genetic Revolution: Science, Myth, and Culture,* ed. Sheldon Krimsky and Kathleen Sloan (New York: Columbia Univ. Press, 2011.

Zornow, William Frank, *Kansas: A History of the Jayhawk State* (Norman: Univ. of Oklahoma Press, 1957).

162

Newspaper Articles and Other Sources

ACLU, "Voting Rights in Indian Country: A Special Report of the Voting Rights Project of the American Civil Liberties Union," 2009.

Adams, Alexis Marie, "Site recalls WWII fear, injustice," *The Boston Sunday Globe*, June 7, 2015, M6.

Andalusia (Firenze, Italy: Bonechi, 2002) (collaborative work).

Balz, Dan and Scott Clement, "On racial issues, America is divided both black and white and red and blue," *The Washington Post*, online Dec. 27, 2014: http://www.washingtonpost.com/politics/on-racial-issues-america-is-divided-both-black-and-white-and-red-and-blue/2014/12/26/3d2964c8-8d12-11e4-a085-34e9b9f09a58_story.html?hpid=z4 .

Graham, Renée, "The world of Ta-Nehisi Coates," *The Boston Globe*, Oct. 20, 2015, p. A8.

Graham, Ruth, "Almost Human," *The Boston Globe*, Feb. 15, 2015, p. K1, K4.

Hemings, Madison, "Life among the Lowly, No. 1," *Pike County Republican*, Pike County, Ohio, March 13, 1873.

Hoban, Virgie, "Researchers suggest another ancestry for Native Americans," *The Boston Globe,* July 22, 2015, p. A1.

Hodge, John L., "For starters, let's agree that there is no 'white America' or 'black America,'" *The Boston Sunday Globe*, Aug. 24, 2014, K12.

Kranish, Michael, "Old battle lines drawn anew in Kansas," *The Boston Sunday Globe*, April 26, 2015, p. A1.

Pace v. Alabama, 106 U.S. 583 (1883).

Proceeding and Acts of the General Assembly of Maryland (September, 1664).

Schworm, Peter, "SAT losing favor as more colleges end requirement," The Boston Globe, Nov. 6, 2015, p. A1.

Seelye, Katherine Q., "Rhode island Church Taking Unusual Step to Illuminate Its Slavery Role," *The New York Times,* Aug. 24, 2015, p. A9.

Shirt v. Hazeltine, U.S. District Court, District of South Dakota, 336 F. Supp. 2d 976 (D.S.D. 2004), 1018 – 1034.

Showboat, a play written by Oscar Hammerstein II based on a novel by Edna Ferber with music by Jerome Kern.

Somerset v Stewart (1772) 98 ER 499; 12 Geo. 3.

The Boston Globe, "SJC's new rule on witnesses should help ensure justice," Jan. 14, 2015, p. A10.

The Constitution of the United States.

The Economist, "American Baptists: Dipped in controversy," June 13, 2015 p. 80.

The Economist, "Breaking the code," Aug. 8, 2015, p. 71.

The Economist, "Civil-war memorials: Too big to veil," July 25, 2015, p. 24.

The Economist, "Dirty sheets and stray cats," June 20, 2015, p. 48.

The Economist, "Ecce Homo naledi," Sept. 12, 2015, p. 76.

The Economist, "From the hood to Harvard," May 2, 2015, p. 26.

The Economist, "Greater than the sum of its parts," Oct. 31, 2015, p. 75.

The Economist, "Guilt and reconciliation," May 2, 2015, p. 44.

The Economist, "Live together, vote together," Nov. 22, 2014, p. 29.

The Economist, "Magna Carta at 800: The uses of history," Dec. 20, 2014, pp. 34 ff.

The Economist, "Nothing idyllic," January 11, 2014, p. 42.

The Economist, "On your toes," April 18, 2015, p. 78.

The Economist, "Probing the chamber of secrets," June 21, 2014, p. 75.

The Economist, "Science's great leap forward," July 7, 2012, p. 13.

The Economist, "The mosque in the cathedral," Oct. 10, 2015.

The Economist, "The power of words," Oct. 17, 2015, p. 90.

The Economist, "Their own worst enemy," Nov. 7, 2015, p. 79.

The Economist, "University challenge," January 17, 2015, pp. 74–75.

The Economist, "Voting with your wallet," Sept. 13, 2014, p. 38.

INDEX

THE AUTHOR

John L. Hodge writes about our roles in advancing or frustrating the growth of democracy. He is the principal co-author of *Cultural Bases of Racism and Group Oppression: An Examination of Traditional "Western" Concepts, Values and Institutional Structures Which Support Racism, Sexism and Elitism* (1975). He is the author of "Democracy and Free Speech: A Normative Theory of Society and Government," Chapter 5 of *The First Amendment Reconsidered* (1982); "Equality: Beyond Dualism and Oppression," Chapter 6 of *Anatomy of Racism* (1990); *How We Are Our Enemy—And How to Stop: Our Unfinished Task of Fulfilling the Values of Democracy* (2011); and *Dialogues on God: Three Views* (2012). He has an A.B. in mathematics from the University of Kansas (where he was awarded membership into Phi Beta Kappa), a Ph.D. in philosophy from Yale University, and a law degree (J.D.) from the University of California, Berkeley (Boalt Hall). In his long career beginning in the mid-1960s he was a draft counselor and peace intern with the American Friends Service Committee in Houston and Seattle; a college teacher and university professor mostly at California State University, East Bay; a Law Clerk for the Massachusetts Appeals Court; a Staff Attorney for the U. S. Court of Appeals for the First Circuit; and a lawyer for Massachusetts state agencies that provided health care, including Medicaid. He participated in the development of the Massachusetts model that was used nationally to create the Affordable Care Act (known as "Obamacare"). He lives with his wife in the Boston area.

For more information, go to http://JohnLHodge.com.

CPSIA information can be obtained
at www.ICGtesting.com
Printed in the USA
FFOW02n0429180116
20443FF